Query Store for SQL Server 2019

Identify and Fix Poorly Performing Queries

Tracy Boggiano
Grant Fritchey

Query Store for SQL Server 2019: Identify and Fix Poorly Performing Queries

Tracy Boggiano
Cary, NC, USA

Grant Fritchey
Grafton, MA, USA

ISBN-13 (pbk): 978-1-4842-5003-7
https://doi.org/10.1007/978-1-4842-5004-4

ISBN-13 (electronic): 978-1-4842-5004-4

Managing Director, Apress Media LLC: Welmoed Spahr
Acquisitions Editor: Jonathan Gennick
Development Editor: Laura Berendson
Coordinating Editor: Jill Balzano

Cover image designed by Freepik (www.freepik.com)

Distributed to the book trade worldwide by Springer Science+Business Media New York, 233 Spring Street, 6th Floor, New York, NY 10013. Phone 1-800-SPRINGER, fax (201) 348-4505, e-mail orders-ny@springer-sbm.com, or visit www.springeronline.com. Apress Media, LLC is a California LLC and the sole member (owner) is Springer Science + Business Media Finance Inc (SSBM Finance Inc). SSBM Finance Inc is a **Delaware** corporation.

For information on translations, please e-mail rights@apress.com, or visit http://www.apress.com/rights-permissions.

Apress titles may be purchased in bulk for academic, corporate, or promotional use. eBook versions and licenses are also available for most titles. For more information, reference our Print and eBook Bulk Sales web page at http://www.apress.com/bulk-sales.

Any source code or other supplementary material referenced by the author in this book is available to readers on GitHub via the book's product page, located at www.apress.com/9781484250037. For more detailed information, please visit http://www.apress.com/source-code.

Printed on acid-free paper

I would like to dedicate this book to my Uncle Elden. He bought me my first two computer books when I was in seventh grade on MS-DOS and QBasic igniting my passion for working on computers. In writing my first technical book, it seems fitting to recognize that without his contribution to my early learning on computers, I may not have stuck with my dreams of becoming involved in the computer field.

—Tracy Boggiano

Table of Contents

About the Authors

Tracy Boggiano Senior Database Administratior for DocuSign has more than 20 years experience on SQL Server and is a speaker at several events including local users groups, virtual groups, SQLSaturdays, and PASS Summit. Her passion outside of computers is volunteering with foster kids as their advocate in court through the North Carolina Guardian ad Litem program.

Grant Fritchey Microsoft Data Platform MVP, has more than 20 years of experience in IT. That time was spent in technical support, development, and database administration. He currently works as Product Evangelist at Red Gate Software.

About the Technical Reviewer

Michael Wells is an engineer at Dell EMC in the Azure Stack product group. He has worked in IT since 2000 and has supported SQL Server since SQL Server 2000. Michael has been active in the SQL Server and .NET Development communities since 2007 and regularly speaks at local user groups, CodeCamps, SQLSaturday events, IT Pro Camps, and large conferences like PASS Summit, Microsoft Ignite, and Oracle OpenWorld.

Introduction

This book is about the Query Store feature built into SQL Server 2019 and how it works to help you identify poorly performing queries and fix them in your databases. Query Store has been in SQL Server since SQL Server 2016 and has gradually added features with each new release to make it better at what information it captures and how it is captured. This book is intended for SQL Server DBAs looking for how Query Store works, the best way to implement it, and how to effectively use it to solve problems. Query Store shows you in an aggregrated form of what was and is running in your database.

Chapter 1 gives you an introduction to how you troubleshoot problems and gather statistics without Query Store, so you gain an understanding of why Query Store is an important new feature of SQL Server. Chapter 2 gives you an overview of how Query Store works and dives into the details of the architecture of it. It covers how the data is captured and where that data is stored. Chapter 3 covers how to configure Query Store and best practices for configuration including trace flags. Chapter 4 covers the six reports that are available for Query Store in SQL Server Management Studio and how to leverage them to get information you need. Chapter 5 dives into detailing what data is available in the catalog views for Query Store.

Chapter 6 covers different use cases for Query Store including using it to show you what is normal performance on your database, troubleshooting query performance and regressed queries, establishing a baseline for your database, and testing upgrades to different versions of SQL Server. Chapter 7 starts showing the real power in Query Store by showing how to identify poorly performing queries and what goes into forcing a plan to stabilize performance. Chapter 8 shows us the most powerful feature, Automatic Plan Regession Correction (APRC), where Query Store automatically forces plans for you. It also introduces to the feature of capturing wait statistics into categories. Chapter 9 shows you techniques to troubleshoot issues with Query Store itself, wait statistics and extended events. Chapter 10 introduces you to two community tools dbatools and sp_blitzQueryStore that help with the configuration of Query Store and getting data out of Query Store.

CHAPTER 1

What Is Query Store?

Query Store keeps rolled-up aggregates of queries and statistics for workloads that are run against your SQL Server database when it is enabled. This data can be used to help you establish a baseline for performance, troubleshoot performance issues, and stabilize performance on your database. In this chapter, we go over techniques that were used before Query Store was released, including Profiler/server-side traces, Extended Events, DMVs (Dynamic Management Views), plan guides, and sp_whoisactive. Then, we will look at how and why Query Store is a game changer for doing these activities.

Query Store is like a flight recorder box for your SQL Server. Query Store stores statistics such as duration, reads, writes, CPU, etc. along with query plans in memory and then aggregates this information based on the settings that were set when Query Store was enabled on the database, with a default of 1 hour. At specified periods, the default is 15 minutes, this data is persisted to disk into the catalog views for you to query or view via the built-in reports in SQL Server Management Studio (SSMS). With the introduction of SQL Server 2017, we also can utilize the power of auto plan correction and the aggregation of wait statistics – more on this in Chapter 8.

This is where the true power of Query Store comes into play. Before this data was only available if you captured it using various other methods that proved to be much slower and cumbersome to work with. To get a better understanding of what Query Store is doing under the covers, we will explore these other methods:

1) Query Store Usefulness

2) Troubleshooting Without Query Store Techniques

3) Query Store: The Game Changer

© Tracy Boggiano and Grant Fritchey 2019
T. Boggiano and G. Fritchey, *Query Store for SQL Server 2019*, https://doi.org/10.1007/978-1-4842-5004-4_1

Query Store Usefulness

Query Store has more than one way it can be utilized to help with your database. In this section, we will discuss how it can be used to help you establish a baseline for your database, troubleshoot performance issues, and stabilize performance.

Baselining Performance

One key part of any database professional's job is being able to baseline the performance of their database server which is not an easy task. In this section of the book, we will talk about the why and how of establishing a baseline for your database server and its relation to Query Store. Query Store's ability to capture all queries that have executed against your database and record runtime statistics in the database makes it easier to collect the baseline information you need.

What Is a Baseline?

Before we talk about how Query Store can provide you with a baseline, let's discuss what a baseline is. A baseline is established by running a workload against a server and taking metrics in several areas to determine if anything has significantly changed over time. Areas of interest in SQL Server include, but are not limited to, CPU utilization, memory clerk usage, number of reads and writes (physical and logical), query execution times, etc. Baselines should be taken during peak and non-peak times to get an accurate measurement of the overall activity of your server. By having a baseline, you will be able to isolate performance problems better and identify bottlenecks.

How Query Store Provides a Baseline

Query Store aggregates data about queries ran against the database it is enabled on into intervals predefined when you configure it. This data is displayed in a few different reports. One example is the Overall Resource Consumption in Figure 1-1 that shows charts of the last month of duration, execution count, CPU time, and logical reads by default. This report is the best for viewing a baseline of the database.

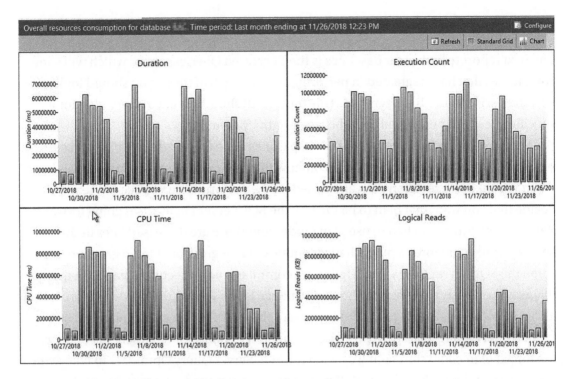

Figure 1-1. *Overall Resource Consumption report*

Catalog Views

All the data collected from Query Store are stored in multiple catalog views. The aggregated runtime statistical data is stored in sys.query_store_runtime_stats. The catalog view sys.query_store_query_text stores unique query text values that have been executed against the database, and the sys.query_context_settings view stores the settings for the queries stored in the sys.query_store_query_text view that was executed under settings such as SET ANSI_NULLS ON or SET QUOTED_IDENTIFERS ON. The view sys.query_store_query stores all queries uniquely executed based on text and context settings executed so you can track them. The sys.query_store_plan catalog view stores the estimated plan for the query executed and the compile time statistics in XML format. The sys.query_store_runtime_stats_interval view stores the time intervals that the data is stored in.

More details on catalog views will be discussed in Chapter 5.

Stabilizing Performance

The next report to look at for baselines is the Regressed Queries report, which will show you queries that have regressed in performance. For each of these, you should look at why the performance has degraded. This report will show how each query plan for a specific query has performed over the last month by default.

From the Regressed Query report or Top Consuming Queries report, you can easily see what plans should be forced based on how they are performing. Forcing a plan is when you take an execution plan and based on the performance you see in the report decide that you want that plan to be the one the SQL Server engine uses going forward. Before Query Store, you had to use plan guides and those are discussed later in this chapter. You would force a plan when you notice plan regression. Plan regression is when the SQL Server Query Plan Optimizer compiles a new execution plan for a query that was previously running and the performance is worse than the previous plan. When a plan is forced manually, you should be aware that no other execution plan will be used for that query going forward. Also, if there is an index change or table schema change, the forced plan could start failing causing the SQL Server Query Optimizer to take extra steps to get an execution plan each time the query is executed. The reports provide a button by which you can force the plans, but you can also for change management purposes use T-SQL to force plans with the stored procedure `sys.sp_force_plan`.

The High Variation report shows you which queries are inconsistent in performance which gives you a way to tell which queries are performing differently at times and may need to be tuned to perform consistently.

SSMS has a Forced Plan report where you track and verify that any plans that were forced are performing as expected.

Tip   Older query plans will be deleted from Query Store based on your settings for retaining query plans, so you may want to keep separate documentation of the performance you expect to see going forward for any forced plans.

Reports will be discussed in greater detail in Chapter 4.

Troubleshooting Without Query Store Techniques

Without Query Store, there are several techniques you can use to troubleshoot problems related to bad query performance. Here we will discuss using SQL Server Profiler to run a trace on the server through the application, running a server-side trace to a file by creating a script using SQL Server Profiler, using Extended Events, pulling information from the DMVs, using a community stored procedure called sp_whoisactive, and using wait statistics.

SQL Server Profiler

SQL Server Profiler is a common tool that collects information about what is running on the server at the moment the application is being executed. Figure 1-2 shows the user interface for it. SQL Server Profiler is used to capture data for short periods of time quickly. It comes with templates to help capture data and gives you the ability to save the data to file or table in a database for later analysis. You must have the ALTER TRACE permission to run SQL Server Profiler.

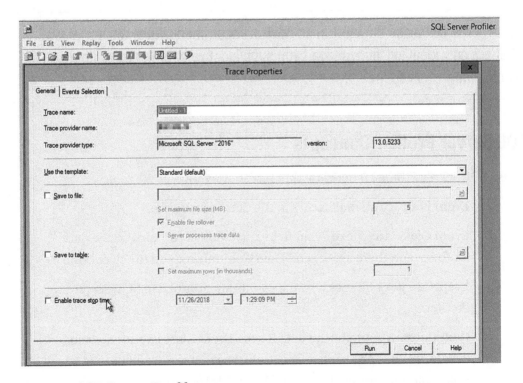

Figure 1-2. *SQL Server Profiler screen*

> **Note**   SQL Profiler and server-side traces as of SQL Server 2017 are being deprecated and are in maintenance mode. They will be removed in a future release of SQL Server in favor of using Extended Events and SSMS XEvent Profiler.

SQL Server Profiler is commonly used in the following use cases:

- Finding slow-running queries and their problem areas.

- Stepping through troublesome queries to find the root cause.

- Capturing a series of events that cause a problem to be replayed on a test system to reproduce the problem.

- Capturing data to compare to performance counters to diagnose problems.

- Capturing a baseline workload to tune workloads. SQL Server Profiler files can be used with the Database Engine Tuning Advisor to recommend indexes and statistics to tune the captured workload.

> **Note**   The Database Engine Tuning Advisor recommends indexes and statistics that are only ideal for the workload you supplied. Evaluate the recommendations, don't blindly apply them.

SQL Server Profiler Concepts

To use SQL Server Profiler, it helps to understand the terms in the tool:

- **Event** is an action that occurs in the database engine.

- **Event Class** is a type of event to be traced. This contains all the data for the event; there are several Data Columns for you to select from.

- **EventCategory** defines how the events are grouped in SQL Server Profiler.

- **Data Column** contains the data for the Event Class captured. Each Event Class has predefined Data Columns that are available. Not all Data Columns are available to all Event Classes.

- **Template** is a predefined trace with an Event Class selected for a particular troubleshooting scenario. A template predefines what events, data columns, and filters to use.

- **Trace** is what SQL Server Profiler runs to capture the selected event classes, data columns, and filters.

- **Filter** is a way to get a subset of data based on criteria that you specify on a Data Column.

Figure 1-3 shows the screen in SQL Server Profiler user to apply filters.

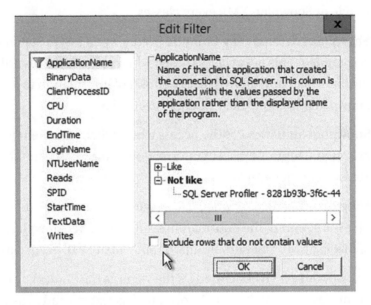

Figure 1-3. *SQL Server Profiler filter screen*

SQL Server Profiler Event Classes Related to Performance

The different event classes that you would use to collect data related to query performance are as follows:

- Under the Performance Event Category:

  - **Auto Stats** occurs when statistics for index or columns are automatically updated. It will also occur when the optimizer loads statistics to be used.

- **Performance Statistics** are used to get the performance statistics of queries, stored procedures, and triggers executing. Six event subclasses construct the lifetime of these actions in the system. Using the subclasses and the following DMVs, you can get the performance history of any query, stored procedure, or trigger: `sys.dm_exec_query_stats`, `sys.dm_exec_procedure_stats`, and `sys.dm_exec_trigger_stats`.

- **Showplan All** occurs when a SQL Statement is executed. It contains a subset of information in the Showplan XML Statistics Profile or Showplan XML event classes.

- **Showplan All for Query Compile** occurs when a SQL Statement is compiled. This event class is used when you want to identify the Showplan operators. This is a subset of information in the Showplan XML for Query Compile event class.

- **Showplan Statistics Profile** occurs when a SQL statement is executed. This is a subset of information in the Showplan XML Statistics Profile event class.

- **Showplan Text** occurs when a SQL statement is executed. This is a subset of the information available in the Showplan All, Showplan XML Statistics Profile, or Showplan XML event classes.

- **Showplan Text (Unencoded)** is the same as the Showplan Text event class, except the data is formatted as text instead of as binary data.

- **Showplan XML** occurs when a SQL statement is executed. This event class is used when you want to identify the Showplan operators. The data in this event class is a defined XML document.

- **Showplan XML for Query Compile** occurs when a SQL statement is compiled. This event class is used when you want to identify the Showplan operators.

- **Showplan XML Statistics Profile** occurs when a SQL statement is compiled. This event class is used when you want to identify the Showplan operators. This event class records complete, compile-time data.

Tip   For all Showplan event classes, limit the number of them in use, because they can cause significant performance overhead. Showplan Text or Showplan Text (Unencoded) are the event classes that will affect performance the least but still should be used sparingly.

- **Plan Guide Successful** has three conditions that have to be true for this event to fire:

  1. The batch or module in the plan guide definition must match the batch or module that is being executed.

  2. The query in the plan guide definition must match the query that is being executed.

  3. The compiled query honors the hints in the plan guide.

- **Plan Guide Unsuccessful** occurs when a plan guide unsuccessfully produces an execution plan. Three conditions have to be true for this event to fire:

  1. The batch or module in the plan guide definition must match the batch or module that is being executed.

  2. The query in the plan guide definition must match the query that is being executed.

  3. The compiled query did not honor the hints in the plan guide.

Note   There is more on how to use plan guides later in this chapter.

- Under the Stored Procedures Event Category:

  - **SP:Completed** occurs when a stored procedure finishes executing.

- **SP:Starting** occurs when a stored procedure starts executing.

- **SP:StmtCompleted** occurs when a T-SQL statement inside the stored procedure finishes executing.

- **SP:StmtStarting** occurs when a T-SQL statement inside the stored procedure starts executing.

- Under the T-SQL Event Category:

  - **SQL:BatchCompleted** occurs when a T-SQL batch finishes executing.

  - **SQL:BatchStarting** occurs when a T-SQL batch starts executing.

  - **SQL:StmtCompleted** occurs when a T-SQL statement finishes executing.

  - **SQL:StmtStarting** occurs when a T-SQL statement starts executing.

In Figure 1-4 you can see the trace properties screen from SQL Profiler.

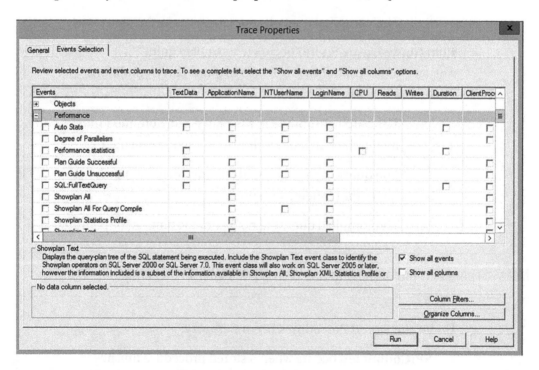

Figure 1-4. *SQL Server Profiler Event Class screen*

Server-Side Traces

Server-side traces are a way to run a SQL Server Profiler session without running the SQL Server Profiler application. This is preferred over running SQL Profiler. You use system stored procedures to specify all the events, data columns, and filters for the trace to capture. You use SQL Profiler to create a script for a server-side trace by opening SQL Server Profiler and specify events and columns you want to capture. Then go under the File menu and select, then Export ➤ Script Trace Definition ➤ For SQL Server 2005 – 2016. (Figure 1-5 shows an example of selecting that menu item).

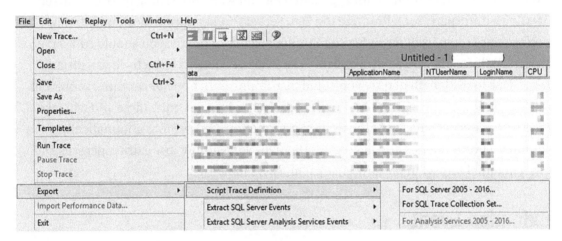

Figure 1-5. *Script out server-side trace definition from SQL Server Profiler*

Server-side traces are considered in maintenance mode, meaning they are planned to be removed in a future version of SQL Server. Thus, you should be trying to switch to Extended Events, which we discuss next.

The list of system stored procedures used to create a server-side trace is as follows:

- sp_trace_create – creates the trace.

- sp_trace_generated_event – creates a user-defined even in SQL Server.

- sp_trace_setevent – adds and removes Data Columns to the trace. You must specify the Event Number. A complete list can be found online at https://docs.microsoft.com/en-us/sql/relational-databases/system-stored-procedures/sp-trace-setevent-transact-sql?view=sql-server-2017.

- `sp_trace_set_filter` – applies a filter to a trace.

- `sp_trace_setstatus` – stops and starts a trace based on the id of the trace you specify. You can query `sys.traces` to find your id.

Disadvantages of SQL Server Profiler or Server-Side Traces over Query Store

A few disadvantages to SQL Profiler or server-side traces over Query Store when getting a baseline are that the data is not aggregated for you with you writing queries yourself or using a third-party tool. Running the SQL Server Profiler application can be a big performance hit in itself to your system under heavy workloads; you should run server-side traces instead if you are not going to use Extended Events (which we will discuss next). Due to the length of time you could be running either one to capture every event, the files or data in the SQL Server Profiler application can get quite large and will take time to process the data to get the desired information. Query Store automatically captures all your queries and aggregates them for you without any extra processes and has a minimal impact in performance on most systems.

Extended Events

Extended Events was introduced in SQL Server 2008 and are a more lightweight way alternative to server-side traces. Extended Events can provide you with more insight into the database engine than SQL Server Profiler and server-side traces. In Figure 1-6, you can see with the newest version of SSMS, you have two built-in Extended Events under the tree labeled XEvent Profiler. One thing to note is once you start a session, they do not stop running when you close SSMS, you must manually stop a session. You can stop can XEvent Profiler session by hitting the red stop button on the toolbar before exiting SSMS.

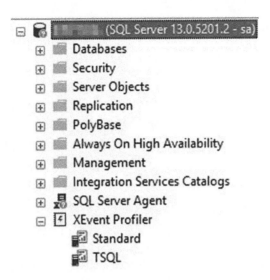

Figure 1-6. *XEvent Profiler in SSMS*

Session definitions can be found in your installation path of SSMS, such as C:\
Program Files (x86)\Microsoft SQL Server\140\Tools\Templates\sql\xevent. In
Figure 1-7, you can find a list of the extended event session provided. The T-SQL
template "Captures all Transact-SQL statements that are submitted to SQL Server by
clients and the time issued. Use to debug client applications." The Standard template
is a "Generic starting point for creating a trace. Captures all stored procedures and
Transact-SQL batches that are run. Use to monitor general database server activity."

Name	Date modified	Type	Size
soft SQL Server › 140 › Tools › Templates › sql › xevent		⌄ ↻	Search xeve
xe_activity.xml	5/17/2017 4:03 AM	XML Document	19 KB
xe_batch_sampling.xml	5/17/2017 4:03 AM	XML Document	5 KB
xe_batch_tracking.xml	5/17/2017 4:03 AM	XML Document	4 KB
xe_connection_tracking.xml	5/17/2017 4:03 AM	XML Document	3 KB
xe_log_io_tracking.xml	5/17/2017 4:03 AM	XML Document	4 KB
xe_Profiler_SP_Counts.xml	5/17/2017 4:03 AM	XML Document	2 KB
xe_Profiler_Standard.xml	5/17/2017 4:03 AM	XML Document	6 KB
xe_Profiler_TSQL.xml	5/17/2017 4:03 AM	XML Document	4 KB
xe_Profiler_TSQL_Duration.xml	5/17/2017 4:03 AM	XML Document	3 KB
xe_Profiler_TSQL_Locks.xml	5/17/2017 4:03 AM	XML Document	8 KB
xe_Profiler_TSQL_Replay.xml	5/17/2017 4:03 AM	XML Document	13 KB
xe_Profiler_TSQL_Sps.xml	5/17/2017 4:03 AM	XML Document	6 KB
xe_Profiler_Tuning.xml	5/17/2017 4:03 AM	XML Document	4 KB
xe_query_lock_counts.xml	5/17/2017 4:03 AM	XML Document	2 KB
xe_query_wait_stats.xml	5/17/2017 4:03 AM	XML Document	13 KB
xe_statement_sample.xml	5/17/2017 4:03 AM	XML Document	8 KB
xe_statement_tracking.xml	5/17/2017 4:03 AM	XML Document	7 KB

Figure 1-7. *Template directory for extended events templates included with SSMS*

Extended Events Concepts

To use Extended Events, it helps to understand the terms used to define them.

- **Packages** contain objects used for getting and processing data for an Extended Events session. Packages can contain the following:

  - **Events** are points that you want to monitor in the execution path of the SQL Server. They can be asynchronous or synchronous. To get a list of events that correspond to the Event Classes in SQL Server Profiler, you can execute the query shown in Listing 1-1.

Listing 1-1. Code to get a list of corresponding Extended Events for SQL Profiler Events

```
USE MASTER;
GO;

SELECT DISTINCT
    tb.trace_event_id,
    te.[name] AS 'Event Class',
    em.package_name AS 'Package',
    em.xe_event_name AS 'XEvent Name',
    tca.[name] AS 'Profiler Category'
FROM (sys.trace_events te
        LEFT OUTER JOIN sys.trace_xe_event_map em
            ON te.trace_event_id =
                em.trace_event_id)
            LEFT OUTER JOIN sys.trace_event_bindings tb
            ON em.trace_event_id = tb.trace_event_id
        INNER JOIN sys.trace_categories tca
            ON tca.category_id = te.category_id
WHERE tb.trace_event_id IS NOT NULL
            AND tca.[name] in ('Stored Procedures',
                                'TSQL',
                                'Performance')
ORDER BY tb.trace_event_id;
```

The same cautions exist as with SQL Server Profiler capturing lots of events, especially with execution plans, can cause performance problems. Below is a list of common events that you may want to capture in an Extended Events session.

- Sp_statement_completed is captured when a statement in a stored procedure completes execution.

- Sql_statement_completed is captured when a SQL statement has completed execution.

- Query_post_compilation_showplan occurs after a SQL statement is compiled and returns the estimated plan in XML format.

- **Targets** tell the session where to store the data.

- **Actions** tell the package what action to take if a certain event happens, such as capturing a stack dump or grabbing an execution plan.

- **Types** are the type of bytes strung together and the length and characteristics of the data to be able to interpret the data. The different types are as follows:

  - event

  - action

  - target

  - pred_source

  - pred_compare

  - type

- **Predicates** are like WHERE clauses to help filter out events that are captured.

- **Maps** is a table that lets you know what an internal value means.

- **Targets** provides a place where the data for a session will be stored.

- **Event counter** is used to keep a count of all events that occurred that you specified for your session synchronously.

- **Event file** writes all event session data from memory to disk asynchronously.

- **Event pairing** determines when paired events do occur in a matched set asynchronously to capture.

- **Event Tracing for Windows (ETW)** correlates events to Windows or applications event data synchronously.

- **Histogram** is used to keep a count of a specified event and occurs asynchronously.

- **Ring buffer** holds data in memory in first-in-first-out (FIFO) method asynchronously.

- **Engine** implements Extended Events by enabling the definition of events, processing event data, managing Extended Events services and objects, and keeping a list of sessions and managing access to the list.

- **Sessions** set up with events in them to collect the information you need to troubleshoot an issue. This pulls everything together to give you the data you need to troubleshoot your issue by allowing to specify actions, targets, and predicates.

Disadvantages of Extended Events over Query Store

Some disadvantages to Extended Events are similar to that of SQL Server Profiler in that the data is not aggregated unless you are doing a single column. It must be run for the entire period of the workload you are measuring which causes the files to get quite large and takes time for you to process the data.

Disadvantage of SQL Server Profiler and Server-Side Traces over Extended Events

SQL Server Profiler and server-side traces process each event that occurs to narrow down to the specific events you have indicated to capture which can cause a performance hit. Due to the performance hit and the lightweight nature of Extended Events it is recommended you use Extended Events. Remember also SQL Server Profiler and server-side traces are being deprecated.

Lightweight Show Plan Trace Flag

Starting in SQL Server 2014, Trace Flag 7412 was introduced to allow to access the actual execution plan of queries that are currently running via the sys.dm_exec_query_ statistics_xml DMV. This data can also be accessed from the Activity Monitor by right-clicking on any running process and selecting Show Live Execution Plan. Improvements were made to make it even more lightweight in SQL Server 2016 SP1. This method is by far more lightweight than capturing the estimated plans with SQL Server Profiler, server-side traces, Extended Events, and Query Store. So, it's recommended you patch your SQL Server instances and enable this trace flag. It is enabled by default in SQL Server 2019. There is a new query hint as well, query_plan_profile, to enable at the query level in

SQL Server 2017 CU11 and SQL Server 2017 CU3. The overhead of enabling this trace flag is estimated to be about a 2% CPU performance hit. Figure 1-8 shows how to show the Live Execution Plan in the Activity Monitor by right-clicking any currently running process.

Note   See this blog post by SQL Server Tiger Team for more information about the performance impacts: `https://bit.ly/2DKR7qg` Also, you can only view the plan while the query is running.

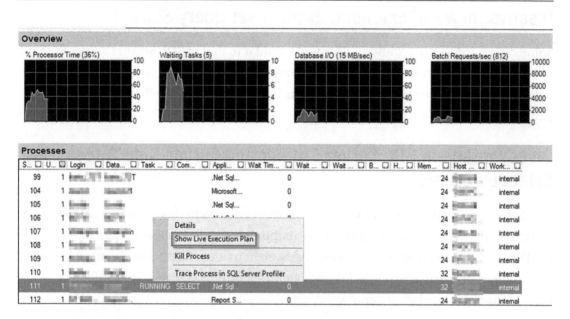

Figure 1-8. *Show Live Execution Plan in Activity Monitor*

sys.dm_exec_query_plan_stats

In SQL Server 2019, DMF (Dynamic Management Function) was introduced which allows you to retrieve the last actual execution plan for a query. This is a compliment to the Lightweight Show Plan Trace Flag above but you don't have to catch the query running to be able to get the execution plan. It requires you to turn on Trace Flag 2451. Then you can run the code in Listing 1-2 to view the execution plan in column last_actual_exec_plan.

Listing 1-2. Query for retrieving last actual execution plan for running processes

```
SELECT er.session_id,
       er.start_time,
       er.status,
       er.command,
       st.text,
       qp.query_plan AS cached_plan,
       qps.query_plan AS last_actual_exec_plan
FROM sys.dm_exec_requests AS er
OUTER APPLY sys.dm_exec_query_plan(er.plan_handle) qp
OUTER APPLY sys.dm_exec_sql_text(er.sql_handle) st
OUTER APPLY sys.dm_exec_query_plan_stats(er.plan_handle) qps
WHERE session_id > 50
       AND status IN ('running', 'suspended');
GO
```

DMVs

Dynamic Management Views (DMVs) were introduced in SQL Server 2005 and made troubleshooting issues with SQL Server easier. There are several DMVs related to performance, but only a few that are related to what is running queries against the SQL Server. We will discuss those DMVs below:

- `sys.dm_exec_cached_plans` stores the estimated execution plan for each query when it is executed until the cache clears it out.

- `sys.dm_exec_connections` contains information about all the connections to the SQL Server. For Azure SQL Database, it returns connections to the SQL Database. It contains relationships with `sys.dm_exec_requests` and `sys.dm_exec_sessions`.

- `sys.dm_exec_cursors` contains information about cursors that are open in the databases on the SQL Server.

- `sys.dm_exec_query_stats` contains aggregated performance data for plans in the plan cache. When the query is purged from the plan cache for any reason, so is the data. Similar to `sys.dm_exec_requests`, this DMV contains the `query_hash` and `query_plan_hash` fields. The `query_hash` field allows you to find queries with same logic. The `query_plan_hash` field allows you to find queries with similar execution plans.

- `sys.dm_exec_procedure_stats` contains aggregated performance data for cached stored procedures in SQL Server. Similar to the above DMV, when the stored procedure's plan is purged from the cache for any reason, so is the data.

- `sys.dm_exec_query_memory_grants` stores information on all queries that have asked for and are waiting for a memory grant or have been granted a memory grant.

- `sys.dm_exec_query_plan` contains the Showplan in XML format for the batch for the `plan_handle` provided.

- `sys.dm_exec_query_stats` contain aggregated performance data for cached query plans in SQL Server. It contains one row per query statement within a plan until a plan is removed from the cache. This DMV contains information on performance including `execution_count`, `worker_time`, `physical_reads`, `logical_writes`, `clr_time`, `elapsed_time`, `rows`, and `dop`. This data is provided in totals, lasts, minimums, and maximums. It also contains information on memory grants, threads, columnstore usage, and tempdb spills. The `query_hash` field can be used to identify queries with same logic and aggregate data together. The `query_plan_hash` field is used to identify similar query plans and sum up the cost of queries with similar plans.

- `sys.dm_exec_requests` shows you each request that is running on the SQL Server. This DMV contains information on performance including `cpu_time`, `reads`, `writes`, `logical_reads`, `row_count`, `wait_time`, and `wait_type`. The `query_hash` field can be used to identify queries with similar logic and aggregate data together. The `query_plan_hash` field is used to identify similar query plans and sum up the cost of queries with similar plans. The `statement_context_id` field is the foreign key for the `sys.query_context_settings` DMV.

- `sys.dm_exec_sessions` contains a row for each session to the SQL Server. It contains information on what is currently running for the session and the resources the session is using.

- `sys.dm_exec_sql_text` contains the text of the SQL batch uniquely identified by the `sql_handle` field. The `sql_handle` field can be used to get information from the following DMVs:

  - `sys.dm_exec_query_stats`

  - `sys.dm_exec_requests`

  - `sys.dm_exec_cursors`

  - `sys.dm_exec_xml_handles`

  - `sys.dm_exec_query_memory_grants`

  - `sys.dm_exec_connections`

The `plan_handle` field can be used to uniquely identify the query plan for a batch from the plan cache and obtain information from the following DMVs:

  - `sys.dm_exec_cached_plans`

  - `sys.dm_exec_query_stats`

  - `sys.dm_exec_requests`

- `sys.dm_exec_xml_handles` contains information about active handles that are open from using `sp_xml_preparedocument`.

Disadvantages of DMVs

There are some disadvantages to using DMVs over Query Store. One is that the data is not persisted to disk; it is only in memory. So, if you restart SQL Server, the data is lost for troubleshooting purposes. Two, the plan cache is allocated memory and plans will be purged from the cache as needed to make room for new plans, so you lose the ability to see everything that has run on the server since it was started. Lastly, you have to build some system to persist the data to disk yourself and to analyze it to get the most value out of the data over time.

sp_whoisactive

sp_whoisactive is a stored procedure written by Adam Machanic that is very useful in capturing information from several DMVs. The procedure and several blog posts about how to use can be found at http://WhoIsActive.com. This procedure combines the DMVs discussed above all into one stored procedure with parameters for you to able to pull back different information. This is useful for getting the estimated plans for processes that are running on your system at the moment. One useful trick is to capture this data into a table periodically, such as every minute, so that you capture long running queries that you can troubleshoot. Article number 25 in the blog series on the web site describes how to capture the data into a table. In Listing 1-3 you will find code with some recommended parameters for capturing the text of the query and execution plans in XML format, along with other useful information, including wait statistics, which will talk about next:

Listing 1-3. Recommended parameters for running sp_whoisactive into a table for troubleshooting

```
EXEC dbo.sp_WhoIsActive
     @get_plans = 1,
     @get_full_inner_text = 1,
     @format_output = 0,
     @get_task_info = 2,
     @destination_table = 'DBA.dbo.WhoIsActiveOutput';
```

There are several other parameters you may find useful to explore all the articles and decide for yourself what is most beneficial for you. There is a @help parameter that prints out documentation of all the parameters.

Wait Statistics

Wait statistics provide another way to troubleshoot what is happening on your SQL Server. Wait statistics were introduced in SQL Server 2005 and offered us a whole new way of troubleshooting. Wait statistics essentially tell you what the database engine is waiting on when it is trying to do work. Wait statistics are in two categories: signal waits and resource waits. When SQL Server is waiting on a thread to become available, it considered a signal wait; this usually indicates that the CPU is running high on the server. Other waits are considered resource waits, such as waiting for the lock of a page. There are hundreds of resource waits. Wait statistics can be queried from the DMV `sys.dm_os_wait_stats`. With this information, you are to tell what your queries are waiting on to execute. You can't tell by an individual query, but with the introduction of Query Store, you will see later it will accumulate per query.

Tip   There is a library online that explains all the wait types available from SQLskills at the following URL: `www.sqlskills.com/help/waits/`. A query that will show you the percent of each wait statistics that has been used since SQL Server was started is available on Paul Randal's blog at `https://bit.ly/2wsQHQE`.

Stabilizing Performance Before Query Store Techniques

There were a few ways to stabilize the performance of query plans before Query Store was introduced in SQL Server 2016. One way was to use plan guides and the `USE PLAN` hint with the query. A second was to keep your statistics up to date as best as possible to ensure the optimizer had the best data available to create a plan. Another was to UPDATE STATISTICS hoping SQL Server would create a better query plan on next execution. Then you also could recompile a stored procedure or function to get to see if SQL Server would generate a better plan. Lastly, you could remove a plan from the cache so that a new plan would be created the next time the query was executed to see if a better plan was created.

Plan Guides/USE PLAN Hint

Plan guides are used to stabilize the performance of a query when you cannot or do not want to change the query. Plan guides work by influencing the optimizer by using query hints or a fixed query plan. Third-party applications can benefit from the use of plan guides because you cannot change the queries. To use a plan guide, you specify the T-SQL you want to optimize and provide query hints for the specific query to use, and SQL Server will match the text of the T-SQL and use the hints when executing that statement. Specifying the plan guide is done using the `OPTION` clause on the query.

There are different types of plan guides:

- OBJECT plan guides

- This type of plan guide matches to object types, such as stored procedures, scalar user-defined functions, multi-statement table-valued user-defined functions, and DML triggers.

- SQL plan guides

    This type of plan guide matches queries based on the T-SQL you provide. They must be parameterized in the correct format. They have to match exactly down the spacing. They apply to stand-alone T-SQL and batches.

- TEMPLATE plan guides

    This type of plan guide matches stand-alone queries parameterized to a certain form. They are used to override a database PARAMETERIZATION option. They can create in the following situations:

    - When the database SET option for PARAMETERIZATION is set to FORCED, but you want queries to compile using the rules for Simple Parameterization.

    - And when you want the opposite effect, the database SET option for PARAMETERIZATION is SIMPLE and you are to use Forced Parameterization.

Plan guide matching occurs at the database level. For SQL or TEMPLATE-based plan guides, SQL Server matches the parameters @module_or_batch and @params to a query character by character.

When you create a plan guide, it will remove the current plan from the plan cache. When you create an OBJECT or SQL plan guide for a batch, SQL Server removes the query plan that has the same hash value. When you create a TEMPLATE plan guide, SQL Server removes all the single-statement batches in the plan cache for that database.

After you create a plan guide, you use the OPTION clause to specify the USE PLAN parameter to specify a query hint.

Listing 1-4 is the original query:

Listing 1-4. A SELECT statement for USE PLAN

```
SELECT count(*) AS Total
FROM Sales.SalesOrderHeader h
      INNER JOIN Sales.SalesOrderDetail d
           ON h.SalesOrderID = d.SalesOrderID
GO
```

Listing 1-5 is the same query with the USE PLAN query hint specified:

Listing 1-5. A USE PLAN Example

```
SELECT count(*) AS Total
FROM Sales.SalesOrderHeader h
      INNER JOIN Sales.SalesOrderDetail d
           ON h.SalesOrderID = d.SalesOrderID
OPTION (USE PLAN N'
<ShowPlanXML xmlns=
"http://schemas.microsoft.com/sqlserver/2004/07/showplan" Version="0.5"
Build="9.00.1187.07">
  <BatchSequence>
    <Batch>
      <Statements>
        ...
      </Statements>
    </Batch>
  </BatchSequence>
</ShowPlanXML>
')
GO
```

Updating Statistics

Using UPDATE STATISTICS to update statistics for a table or index can help improve performance if you know a lot of data has changed in the table or index. Beware that updating statistics does recompile all the plans that the table or index are referenced in, so you will not want to do this too frequently unless necessary. Prior to SQL Server 2014, 20% of a table had to be updated before the auto updated statistic would be triggered unless you used Trace Flag 2371 which was introduced in SQL Server 2008 SP1 to lower this; 20% is not ideal for large tables such as data warehouse tables. In SQL Server 2016, this trace flag is on by default.

To update statistics for a table, use Listing 1-6.

Listing 1-6. UPDATE STATISTICS for a table

```
USE DATABASE;
GO
UPDATE STATISTICS SchemaName.TableName;
GO
```

To update statistics for a particular index, use Listing 1-7.

Listing 1-7. UPDATE STATISTICS for an index

```
USE DATABASE;
GO
UPDATE STATISTICS SchemaName.TableName IndexName;
GO
```

Recompiling Stored Procedures

Whenever you can identify a stored procedure, trigger, or function that is performing poorly due to parameter sniffing or other issues, you can use sp_recompile to recompile the object on the next execution of the procedure. Parameter sniffing occurs when an execution plan is generated that is optimal for one workload, but not optimal for all workloads based on the parameters used for the query. Running this procedure will effectively remove the current plan from the plan cache so a new plan can be compiled on the next execution of the query. The new plan may be the same as the old plan though depending on the parameters passed in.

Removing Plans from the Plan Cache

You can query sys.dm_exec_cached_plans and sys.dm_exec_sql_text to retrieve a plan handle to remove a specific plan from the cache that is not part of a stored procedure, function, or trigger by using the following code.

First, in Listing 1-8 you select the text you need to find that is part of your query:

Listing 1-8. Find the plan handle for the SQL text you are looking for

```
SELECT cp.plan_handle, st.
FROM sys.dm_exec_cached_plans AS cp
CROSS APPLY sys.dm_exec_sql_text(plan_handle) AS st
WHERE  LIKE N'%/* MyTable %';
```

Then copy and paste the plan handle into the FREEPROCCACHE procedure in the code provided in Listing 1-9:

Listing 1-9. DBCC FREEPROCCACHE to remove SQL text plan from the plan cache

```
DBCC FREEPROCCACHE (<plan_handle>);
```

Query Store: The Game Changer

Query Store changes how you troubleshoot bad query plans because now everything is collected, stored on disk, and persisted over time to provide you trends in performance. It provides all the estimated plans that have been used in the retention period you have defined which allows you to troubleshoot the query with a graphical interface easily and efficiently. Query Store changes how you can troubleshoot performance, baseline your system, and stabilize the performance of your SQL Server significantly.

What Information Is Gathered

Query Store gathers runtime statistics for each query that ran and their estimated plans. The following data is collected per query and aggregated per time interval you have specified in SQL Server 2019:

- Execution count
- Duration
- CPU time
- Logical reads
- Logical writes
- Physical reads
- CLR time
- DOP
- Memory consumption
- Row count

Each statistic is available in totals, averages, maximums, minimums, and standard deviations. More information about what data will be discussed in Chapters 4 and 5.

What Information Query Store Provides for Us: Use Cases

There are different use cases for Query Store besides just collecting performance information. They include

- Finding and fixing regressed queries
- Finding and identifying top resource consuming queries
- A/B testing
- Stabilizing performance when upgrading SQL Server
- Finding and identifying ad hoc workloads so you can improve them

These will be discussed in more detail in Chapter 6.

Automatic Plan Correction

SQL Server 2017 introduced Automatic Plan Correction that will automatically force plans and unforce plans based on plan regression. So, you no longer have to force plans, although you still can if necessary manually. Chapter 8 will talk more about how this feature works.

Wait Statistics

SQL Server 2017 introduced wait statistics that are being collected per query in 23 different categories, such as buffer and CPU. A detailed list is provided in Chapter 8 of which wait statistics are in each category. Chapter 8 will talk more about this feature.

Conclusion

Query Store offers an automated and easy way to collect performance information about queries that are running on your SQL Server. There are several use cases for using Query Store besides just seeing performance information. It provides Automatic Plan Correction and wait statistics collection starting in SQL Server 2017, which are invaluable new tools. The rest of the book will go into much more detail about Query Store so you can benefit the most from using it.

CHAPTER 2

Overview and Architecture of the Query Store

In order for the Query Store to collect and maintain a baseline on query performance, it needs an architecture that has minimal impact on the overall performance of SQL Server. This chapter will review how Query Store operates to collect data. We'll also cover the various data sets that make up the Query Store. This information should make it possible for you to both understand what the Query Store is doing and have faith that it's performing these actions in the safest manner possible for your databases.

How Query Store Works

While we are going to cover the data collected in some detail later in the chapter, it makes it easier to understand how Query Store works if we first give a quick overview of the types of data being collected. There are three fundamental data sets that define the Query Store data:

- Query and Plan Information: Data about the query itself and about the execution plans derived from that query by the query optimizer.

- Query Runtime Information: This is the information about how fast the query ran and how many times it was called, along with other performance-related information from query execution.

- Query Wait Statistics: This information covers the various waits that occurred on a single query during the execution on the server.

T. Boggiano and G. Fritchey, *Query Store for SQL Server 2019*, https://doi.org/10.1007/978-1-4842-5004-4_2

With those core data sets defined, we can now move on to determine exactly where that information comes from and how it gets collected. We will cover all three data sets in much more detail later in the chapter. We will use these data sets as our architecture for describing the ways that Query Store gathers the data because the data sets help define the approach taken by the Query Store. This is why it was important to establish what those data sets are before we talk about where they came from.

On additional detail that you need to know to understand how the Query Store works is that this is a database level setting. It's not controlled on the server, but rather database-by-database in your system. This is an important detail because the information the Query Store captures is written to each individual database, not a central location.

Collecting Query and Plan Information

When a query gets submitted to SQL Server, it runs through a series of processes. These processes ensure that the query is properly written, that the objects in the database referenced by the query actually exist, and, most importantly, that the query is optimized to run quickly. Figure 2-1 shows an overview of this process:

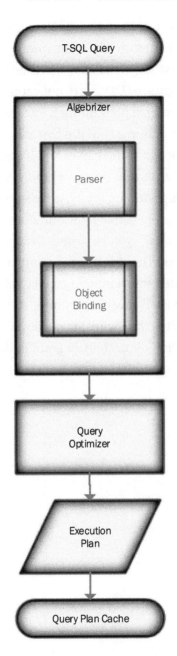

Figure 2-1.   *The basic process of generating an execution plan*

We start with the T-SQL query of course. Only Data Manipulation Language (DML) queries are captured by the Query Store. These are queries that are used to SELECT, UPDATE, DELETE, or INSERT data. Queries that are used to manipulate the data structures, Data Definition Language (DDL), are not captured to the Query Store. When the query first comes to SQL Server, it goes through an internal process called the Algebrizer. This does a number of things, but the two we care about the most are that it validates that the syntax is correct in the parser and it ensures that the objects in the query are actually in the database, through object binding. The Algebrizer also gathers a bunch of information that, along with the query, it passes to the query optimizer.

The query optimizer is the process that determines an efficient way to retrieve or modify your data based on the query you've supplied it and the tables, indexes, statistics, and constraints in your database. The result of the query optimization process itself is an execution plan which gets written into a memory space called the plan cache.

With one exception, which we'll cover in a minute, the Query Store does not interfere with this process in any way. What the Query Store does is capture the output of the processes that create an execution plan. Here's a graphic showing how the Query Store works side-by-side with the query optimization process as you can see in Figure 2-2:

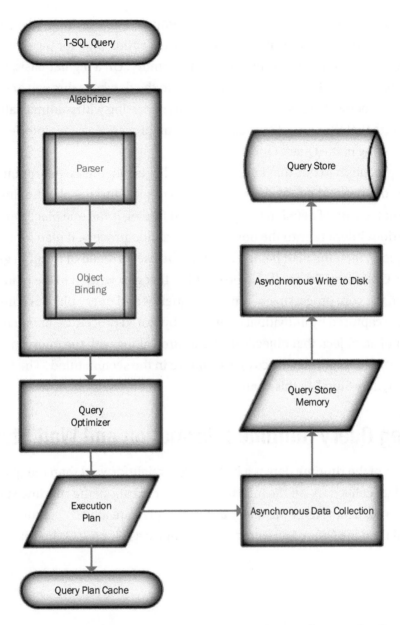

Figure 2-2. *The process of capturing the execution plan and query for the Query Store*

After the query optimizer does its work and generates an execution plan, an asynchronous process captures the query and the execution plan for the query store. It outputs them to a temporary storage space in memory. On a regular basis, the query information stored in memory gets written to the database through another asynchronous process. Microsoft describes this as occurring with minimal latency. The goal is to ensure that the Query Store data collection process does not interfere with the normal processing of the Query Optimizer.

The one exception to this that I mentioned earlier is that the asynchronous process that captures queries and query plans also checks to see if there is plan forcing in place. We'll cover that in a lot of detail in Chapter 7. Plan forcing is the one place where the Query Store does interfere with the normal optimization process. If plan forcing is in place for a query, then the plan being forced will be used instead of the plan generated by the Query Optimizer. That will also be the plan that gets written to the plan cache.

With that, the core processing of retrieving queries and query plans is complete. The information is captured by individual query, not by stored procedure or batch. If the query is part of an object, that object's ID is captured along with the query information. We'll cover the details of what exactly gets capture in the section titled "The Data Collected By Query Store" in this chapter.

Collecting Query Runtime Information and Wait Statistics

The collection of the runtime data is a little more straightforward than the query and query plan data collection. All the information collected about the runtime statistics and wait statistics occurs after the query and query plan are already captured. The query executes and then the Query Store process takes place as Figure 2-3 shows:

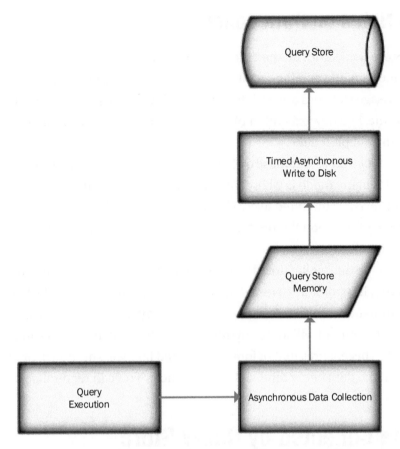

Figure 2-3. *The process of capturing runtime metrics for the Query Store*

There is only one fundamental difference in the processing of this data collection and that of the query and query plan data. This is the timed asynchronous writes to disk. Instead of a process with minimal latency, the data is stored and aggregated in-memory for a period of time. The default is 15 minutes. You can control this and we'll cover it in detail in Chapter 3.

The information, such as how long a query took to run and the waits experienced during the execution, is written to memory. That data is aggregated there in memory. When that information is written to disk, it gets reaggregated based on another setting, the collection interval. By default this is 60 minutes. What this aggregation gives you is the ability to compare two different time periods so that you can see if the performance of a query is changing over time. We'll cover this in more detail in the "Data Collected" section.

General Notes on Data Collection

The Query Store works with all the other processes within SQL Server. So, for example, if a query is recompiling and it generates the same execution plan that is already in the Query Store, usage statistics are updated and nothing else happens. If, however, this recompile results in a new execution plan, then that plan will get captured to the Query Store just as the old plan did.

In the event of a cross-database query using three-part naming, the database from which the call is being made is where the query will be recorded, regardless of where the data being retrieved or modified lives. This is important so that you know where to look for Query Store information if more than one database is involved. You will not see the query in both databases.

Because all the data collection done in the Query Store gets written to disk asynchronously, it is possible to lose data because it has not yet been flushed to disk. There is a command to make this happen manually, `sys.sp_query_store_flush_db`. Executing that command will force anything currently in memory to be immediately written to disk. This ensures that before a controlled failover, shutdown, or any event that would result in the data being removed from memory, you can retain that data.

The Data Collected by Query Store

As we stated at the beginning of the chapter, there are essentially three sets of information that define the data collected by the Query Store: query and plan data, runtime data, and wait statistics. As you saw in the previous section, the runtime data and the wait statistics are collected the same way, so why break them apart? The reason is simple, the focus of the book is SQL Server 2019, but Query Store has been implemented since SQL Server 2016. One change between 2016 and 2017 was the addition of wait statistics in the data collection. So we're breaking that apart just so those who will only see the runtime information still get as much out of the book as those who look at both runtime data and wait statistics. Plus, you'll need to plan on querying the wait statistics slightly differently than you do the runtime data, but we'll cover that in detail in Chapter 5.

One point about the system views that expose the Query Store information must be made. The information displayed in these system views combines, but does not aggregate, the information stored on disk and in memory. As you know from earlier in the chapter, data is written first to memory and then eventually written to disk. During that interval, the runtime data will be aggregated in both places, but visible as separate rows in some of the catalog views. There's nothing you need to do to combine this data. SQL Server does it for you. However, there's also nothing you can do to separate this data. It's combined at the system level.

Let's start with the data collected about the query and the query plan itself.

Query and Query Plan Information

As we've already stated previously, the foundation for the information gathered by Query Store is the query itself. You may pass a batch with five or ten statements, but each of those statements, assuming they're all data manipulation statements, will be individual queries in the Query Store. The catalog views that expose the information available in Query Store are visible in Figure 2-4:

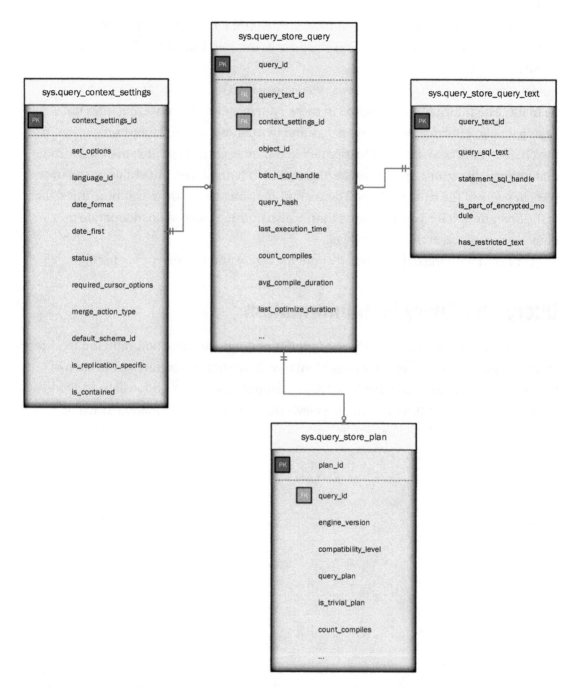

Figure 2-4. *Catalog views containing query and query plan information*

There are only four catalog views that expose the information stored on the query and the query plan. At the top and center, you can see `sys.query_store_query`. In the diagram only a few of the 30 columns are shown as examples of what information is available. Each query has attributes that may or may not be unique to the query. These attributes are the tables to the left and right of `sys.query_store_query`: `sys.query_store_context_settings` and `sys._query_store_query_text`. These attributes can be created once and then reused by multiple queries. This includes the query text. If other attributes change, but the query text remains the same, then more than one query in `sys.query_store_query` may have the same `query_text_id` value (query_id is the primary key). The query plans stored in `sys.query_store_plan` are tied directly to the query via a foreign key on query_id. Any given query may have multiple plans. Situations arise like parameter sniffing and others that result in a given query with more than one valid execution plan. The table shown in Figure 2-4 for `sys.query_store_plan` also only contains a sampling of the 23 columns available.

We'll be covering querying these tables in detail in Chapter 5. However, it's worth pointing out that some of the information may be a little misleading. If you look at both `sys.query_store_query` and `sys.query_store_plan` as shown in Figure 2-4, both have a column labeled `count_compiles`. While these values are labeled the same, they actually represent the difference between the results of a compile or recompile event for a query or for a plan. Every time a query gets compiled or recompiled, that value will be updated appropriately. However, that compile event may, or may not, result in the same plan. If a different plan gets compiled, then that plan gets its own distinct `count_compiles` value updated, not every plan associated with the query. Details like this we'll be addressing throughout the book.

The rows of data stored in `sys.query_store_plan` actually act as the drivers for the runtime data collected. Let's now take a look at that information.

Runtime Information

The runtime data actually gets aggregated based on two different values, the `plan_id` as mentioned in the previous section and the runtime interval that we talked about earlier (that has a default of 60 minutes). Figure 2-5 represents the information captured:

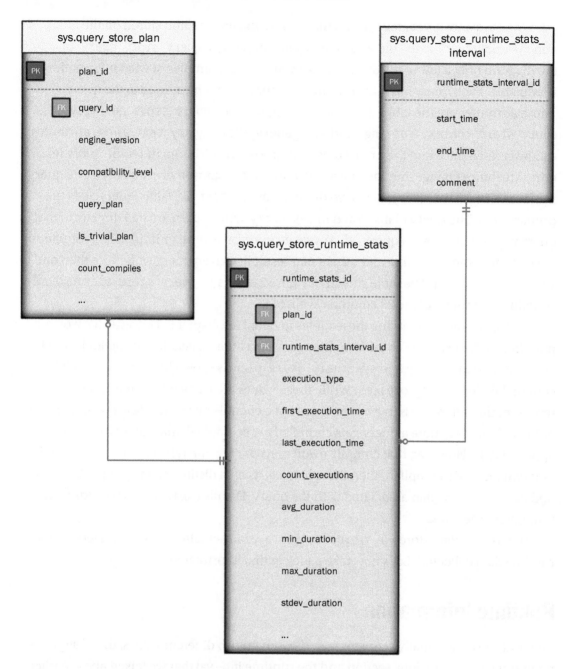

Figure 2-5. *Catalog views containing runtime information*

The model may look quite a bit more simplified, but it masks a few complexities that are worth noting. First up, the sys.query_store_runtime_stats catalog view shows only a small part of the 58 columns that make up the view. A lot of that data is laid out similar to what you see with the duration values: an average, a minimum, a maximum, and a standard deviation. That holds true for such interesting data as the CPU time, row count, memory, and more.

The next most important thing to keep in mind when dealing with the runtime data is that it is broken up into multiple aggregations as determined by the runtime interval. Since you're unlikely to turn Query Store on at the top of the hour, the sys.query_store_runtime_stats_interval system view will have the start_time and end_time of each interval. While these will be the appropriate amount of time apart, 60 minutes by default, the start and stop times are not going to coincide with the clock.

Another thing to remember is that there are multiple time values to take into account with this information. In addition to the runtime interval, there is also the time to flush to disk, with a default of 15 minutes. That means that for any given plan_id, there may be data on disk across multiple time intervals as well as data in memory.

Further, the execution_type can affect the information collected. This column has three values:

- 0 – Successful execution

- 3 – User aborted execution

- 4 – An exception or error causing aborted execution

In the case of a query being aborted for any reason, the runtime data is still collected. However, it's aggregated into a separate value for the given plan_id and for the given runtime_stats_interval_id. Because of this and the fact that there can be more than one row of runtime data between memory and disk, when you start writing your own queries against this data, you need to aggregate based on the plan_id, the execution_type, and the runtime_stats_interval_id.

Wait Statistics

We've separated the wait statistics from the runtime information only because some people using this book may be on SQL Server 2016. Figure 2-6 shows the layout of the information gathered for the wait statistics:

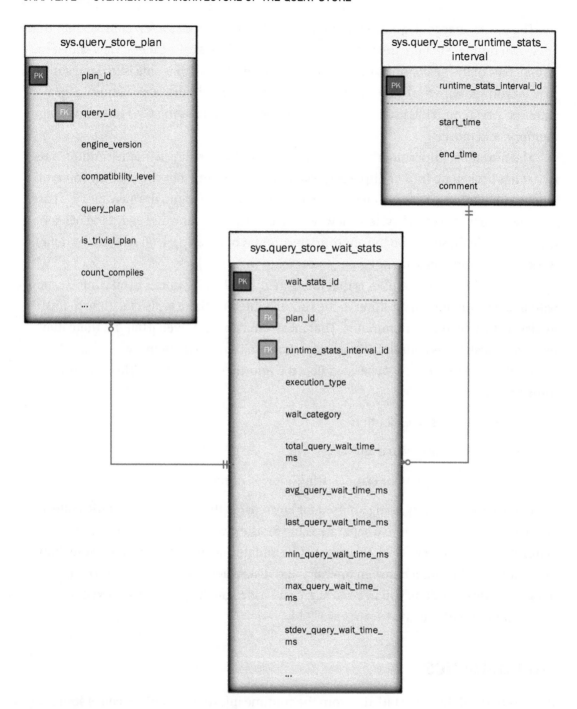

Figure 2-6. *Catalog views contain wait statistics*

Just like with the runtime information, the wait statistics are aggregated by the runtime interval. Also, like the runtime information, wait statistics are dependent on the flush to disk interval, a default of 15 minutes, so will be aggregated in two locations. Again, like the runtime information, the execution_type also affects the aggregation of the wait statistics. Finally, the wait statistics add one more wrinkle. There is a wait_category that must be taken into account when aggregating the data across time intervals and execution_types. We'll be covering all this in more detail in Chapter 5.

You can also see that there is a similar pattern to the data with a minimum, maximum, last, average, and standard deviation being stored. However, the wait time is the only interesting value. I left off a couple of descriptive columns in Figure 2-6 to save space. The rest of the information there is the important data for wait statistics.

Information About the Query Store

There is actually one final catalog view that we should mention, although the details of what it represents will be covered in Chapter 3. That view is sys.database_query_store_options. While it does represent some of the information gathered about the Query Store, it is not the focus of this chapter.

Summary

The principal driving factor of the methodology of collecting query store data is to do so in as unobtrusive a way as possible. All the asynchronous calls between the storage of the information to memory and disk make that abundantly clear. However, once the data is stored to disk, it lives with the database and will be available, wherever that database goes, until it is removed from another process, such as automatic cleanup, or by you manually removing the information. In Chapter 3, we'll finally get going with starting, stopping, and controlling the Query Store.

CHAPTER 3

Configuring Query Store

As with any SQL Server feature, maximizing its potential involves tuning that feature for your specific environment. Common advice would be to begin with the defaults, then compare these with commonly agreed best practices and adjust those to what makes sense for your use case if necessary. Often there will be a widely accepted set of best practices within the community for typical deviations from Microsoft defaults. Sometimes defaults that appear "dumb" are often set that way, not because Microsoft is ignorant of its product or user base but for backward compatibility reasons.

In this chapter, we will discuss the steps for implementing and configuring the Query Store feature. We will cover the default configuration both on-premise and in the Azure SQL Database Platform as a Service (PaaS) offering. There will be a detailed breakdown of all the Query Store configuration options and the Query Store catalog views related to the configuration (for a list of all the Query Store–related catalog views, look to Chapter 5).

After this, we will commence a deep dive into best practices for configuring the Query Store. We will talk about how parameterization and parameterization settings can impact Query Store as well as the impact of renaming objects. Trace flags to improve recovery times and important performance-related patches for versions 2016 and 2017 will also be highlighted.

For those of you leveraging the capabilities of In-Memory OLTP, the use of Query Store with natively compiled stored procedures will be covered. We will also discuss an exciting new feature introduced in SQL 2017, known as automatic plan regression correction (APRC). What it entails and how to enable or disable it will be covered.

We will close the chapter with a discussion of the various query store error states and details on how to maintain the Query Store as a DBA.

© Tracy Boggiano and Grant Fritchey 2019
T. Boggiano and G. Fritchey, *Query Store for SQL Server 2019*, https://doi.org/10.1007/978-1-4842-5004-4_3

Query Store Defaults

In this section, we will look at the default configuration options for the Query Store in SQL Server. Default options in SQL Server are not always the optimal configuration setting for your environment, but changing them does merit careful consideration. An important point to note is that the Query Store is disabled by default in the on-premise product for versions 2016, 2017, and 2019 at time of this writing. However, in the Microsoft Platform as a Service (PaaS) offering Azure SQL Database, it is enabled by default. For Azure SQL Database Managed Instances, a managed Infrastructure as a Service (IaaS) offering, the Query Store is supported but also disabled by default.

To enable Query Store, run the following T-SQL command in Listing 3-1:

Listing 3-1. T-SQL to enable Query Store on a database

```
ALTER DATABASE [<Database Name>] SET QUERY_STORE=ON;
```

To enable Query Store on all databases on your instance you can run the code in Listing 3-2:

Listing 3-2. Turn Query Store on all databases

```
DECLARE @SQL NVARCHAR(MAX) = N'';

SELECT @SQL += REPLACE(N'ALTER DATABASE [{{DBNAME}}] SET QUERY_STORE=ON ',
     '{{DBName}}', [name])
FROM sys.databases
WHERE state_desc = 'ONLINE'
     AND [name] NOT IN ('master', 'tempdb')
ORDER BY [name];

EXEC (@SQL);
```

The Query Store cannot be enabled in either the master or the tempdb system databases. Enabling the Query Store in the *model* database does not actually capture any Query Store data in the *model* database, but this configuration change will be reflected in newly created databases from that point forward. In the msdb system database, the Query Store will behave no differently than the Query Store in a user database. A table of options for Azure SQL Database and regular on-premise SQL server is presented in Table 3-1.

Table 3-1. *Configuration options for Query Store*

Configuration Name	Options	Description	Default
OPERATION_MODE	OFF READ_WRITE READ_ONLY	Mode of operation for the Query Store	OFF (SQL 2016 and 2016) READ_WRITE for Azure SQL Database
CLEANUP_ POLICY(STALE_QUERY_ THRESHOLD_DAYS)	BIGINT	Dictates CLEAN_UP policy (0 is never)	30 days (or 7 for Azure SQL Database Basic Edition)
DATA_FLUSH_ INTERVAL_SECONDS	BIGINT	Flush interval frequency for buffered Query Store data	900 (15 minutes)
MAX_STORAGE_SIZE_ MB	BIGINT	The maximum size of Query Store in MB	100 (SQL Server 2016 and 2017), 1000 (SQL Server 2019), (1024 for SQL Azure Database Premium and 10 for SQL Azure Database Basic Edition)
INTERVAL_LENGTH_ MINUTES	1, 5, 10, 15, 30, 60, or 1440	Aggregation interval for statistics	60
SIZE_BASED_ CLEANUP_MODE	AUTO OFF	Attempt to clean up if approaching capacity	AUTO
QUERY_STORE_ CAPTURE_MODE	AUTO ALL CUSTOM NONE	Query capturing behavior	AUTO (SQL Server 2016 and 2017), ALL (SQL Server 2019) ALL (Azure SQL Database)
MAX_PLANS_PER_ QUERY	INT	How many distinct plans to keep per query	200. Not available in SQL Server 2016
WAIT_STATISTICS_ CAPTURE_MODE	ON OFF	Specifies rather to capture wait statistics for queries	ON in SQL Server 2017 and 2019 and Azure SQL Database. Not available in SQL Server 2016

Configuration Options

Query Store has many options to configure to properly be set up to collect data in the most beneficial way for your database. This section will explain those options and give you recommendations on what the best settings would be and how to set those options. First, we will go through all the options and what they mean and look at code on how to change them. Then we will see what is available in the GUI and how to change options there.

OPERATION_MODE

This setting sets the operational mode of the Query Store. The Query Store operates in either read-only or read and write mode. In read-only mode, existing data will remain in the Query Store, but no new queries will be captured. If the Query Store reaches capacity, it will change from READ_WRITE to READ_ONLY mode. If capturing new queries is desired, which it typically will be, it is important to monitor to ensure that the Query Store has its OPERATION_MODE set correctly. The T-SQL syntax for setting this is in Listing 3-3.

Listing 3-3. T-SQL to set Query Store operation mode

```
ALTER DATABASE [<Database Name>] SET QUERY_STORE ( OPERATION_MODE = READ_
WRITE );
```

The Query Store has the concept of an actual state and the desired state. Where the desired state is READ_WRITE, and the actual state is READ_ONLY, there will be an associated reason which will be displayed in the catalog view sys.database_query_store_options under the column readonly_reason. The associated catalog views for the Query Store will be covered in Chapter 5. The default setting is READ_WRITE.

CLEANUP_POLICY (STALE_QUERY_THRESHOLD_DAYS)

The Query Store has a configurable number of days to store Query Store data. The Query Store settings SIZE_BASED_CLEANUP_MODE and QUERY_STORE_CAPTURE_MODE will also have an impact on the data stored in Query Store, so it is possible for queries that do not exceed the stale threshold not to be stored. The default for STALE_QUERY_THREHOLD_DAYS is 30 days (or 7 days if using Azure SQL Database Basic edition). The T-SQL for configuring this setting is in Listing 3-4.

Listing 3-4. T-SQL to set STALE_QUERY_THRESHOLD_DAYS

```
ALTER DATABASE [<Database Name>] SET QUERY_STORE ( CLEANUP_POLICY = (
STALE_QUERY_THRESHOLD_DAYS = <Value> ) );
```

DATA_FLUSH_INTERVAL_SECONDS

As discussed in Chapter 2, for performance purposes the Query Store will buffer data and write it asynchronously to disk at configurable intervals. This interval is known as the *data flush interval,* and it is specified in seconds. As will be discussed in greater detail in the section on Best Practices, this option requires careful consideration as it can have a considerable impact on the performance of the Query Store. Anyone familiar with indirect checkpoints and target recovery intervals in SQL Server will have a grasp of the trade-offs involved in setting the data flush interval for the Query Store. A short flush interval will result in more aggressive I/O spikes when the Query Store data is flushed to disk. This can lead to performance degradation of the I/O subsystem. A longer data flush interval should allow SQL Server to spread the I/O load over a longer time frame at the expense of greater data loss in the event of a systemic failure (since more of the Query Store data will be held in volatile memory). The default flush interval is 900 seconds (15 minutes). The T-SQL for configuring this setting is in Listing 3-5.

Listing 3-5. T-SQL to set DATA_FLUSH_INTERVAL_SECONDS

```
ALTER DATABASE [<Database Name>] SET QUERY_STORE ( DATA_FLUSH_INTERVAL_
SECONDS = <Value> );
```

MAX_STORAGE_SIZE_MB

This setting determines the maximum storage size for the Query Store data for an individual database in megabytes. The default setting of 1000 MB is quite small for any database with even a moderate level of activity. If this threshold is reached, the Query Store will change state from READ_WRITE to READ_ONLY. Even with SIZE_BASED_ CLEANUP_MODE set to AUTO (more on this later), it is still possible for the Query Store to reach maximum capacity especially during periods of high activity. It is crucial to set the maximum storage size for the Query Store appropriately for your environment, considering your desired history retention set by the STALE_QUERY_THRESHOLD_DAYS value. The T-SQL for configuring this setting is in Listing 3-6:

Listing 3-6. T-SQL to set MAX_STORAGE_MAX_MB

```
ALTER DATABASE [<Database Name>] SET QUERY_STORE ( MAX_STORAGE_SIZE_MB =
<Value> );
```

INTERVAL_LENGTH_MINUTES

The INTERVAL_LENGTH_MINUTES is an important setting as it determines what interval data is aggregated into for viewing later. You can only select from values of 1, 5, 10, 14, 60, and 1440 minutes. The default value is 60 minutes. The smaller the interval, the more disk space it will take up but the more granular data you will have. The T-SQL for configuring this setting is in Listing 3-7.

Listing 3-7. T-SQL to set INTERVAL_LENGTH_MINUTES

```
ALTER DATABASE [<Database Name>] SET QUERY_STORE ( INTERVAL_LENGTH_MINUTES
= <Value> );
```

SIZE_BASED_CLEANUP_MODE

The SIZE_BASED_CLEANUP_MODE default value is AUTO which means it will automatically clean up the data based on the MAX_STORAGE_SIZE_MB and CLEANUP_POLICY settings. The other option is to set it to OFF. This setting is set to tell Query Store to clean up data automatically before reaching the number of days specified with the CLEANUP_POLICY setting if it reaches the MAX_STORAGE_SIZE_MB value first. So, if you set Query Store to keep 30 days of data and it reaches your max size of 2 GB at day 28, it will start purging data at the point and time. The T-SQL for configuring this setting is in Listing 3-8.

Listing 3-8. T-SQL to set SIZE_BASED_CLEANUP_MODE

```
ALTER DATABASE [<Database Name>] SET QUERY_STORE ( SIZE_BASED_CLEANUP_MODE
= <Value> );
```

QUERY_STORE_CAPTURE_MODE

The QUERY_STORE_CAPTURE_MODE default is ALL for both SQL Server on-premise and for Azure SQL Database. Another option is NONE, which tells Query Store to not capture new queries only, it continues to capture runtime statistics for queries that have already been captured by Query Store. The third option AUTO tells SQL Server not to capture queries that do take up significant resources or are not executed often. The T-SQL for configuring this setting is in Listing 3-9.

Listing 3-9. T-SQL to set QUERY_STORE_CAPTURE_MODE

```
ALTER DATABASE [<Database Name>] SET QUERY_STORE ( QUERY_STORE_CAPTURE_MODE
= [<Value>] );
```

For the CUSTOM option for QUERY_STORE_CAPTURE_MODE, there are three options you can use to control how that data will be stored. This option was introduced to help with controlling what data was captured for ad-hoc workloads in SQL Server 2019. The STALE_CAPTURE_POLICY_THRESHOLD accepts a number for days or hours, from 1 hour up to 7 days that a query must exceed on of the values in the next three options in for the data for query to be captured. The three options that control what will be captured in the CUSTOM mode and operate in an OR manner are listed below:

- EXECUTION_COUNT – Specifies how many times a query must be executed in the time period.

- TOTAL_COMPILE_CPU_TIME_MS – Specifies the total CPU compile time a query must use in the time period.

- TOTAL_EXECUTION_CPU_TIME_MS – Specifies the total CPU execution time the query must use in the time period.

The T-SQL for configuring the CUSTOM setting is in Listing 3-10.

Listing 3-10. T-SQL to set QUERY_STORE_CAPTURE_MODE for CUSTOM mode

```
ALTER DATABASE [<Database Name>]
SET QUERY_STORE = ON
    (
      QUERY_CAPTURE_MODE = CUSTOM,
      QUERY_CAPTURE_POLICY = (
        STALE_CAPTURE_POLICY_THRESHOLD = 24 HOURS,
        EXECUTION_COUNT = 30,
        TOTAL_COMPILE_CPU_TIME_MS = 1000,
        TOTAL_EXECUTION_CPU_TIME_MS = 100
      )
    );
```

MAX_PLANS_PER_QUERY

The MAX_PLANS_PER_QUERY default is 200 plans. This setting is not available in SQL Server 2016. That may seem like a large number, but on some systems, there are thousands of plans per query, but 200 is a good starting point. The higher this setting though, the more disk space you will need if you have a large number of queries with a large number of plans. If you notice that you are hitting that limit, you can run the code in Listing 3-11 to see what your max number of query plans currently in plan cache is and use it determine what you would like this setting to be set to.

Listing 3-11. T-SQL to find the number of plans in the cache per query

```
SELECT query_hash,
COUNT (DISTINCT query_plan_hash) distinct_plans
FROM sys.dm_exec_query_stats
GROUP BY query_hash
ORDER BY distinct_plans DESC;
```

The T-SQL for configuring this setting is in Listing 3-12.

Listing 3-12. T-SQL to set MAX_PLANS_PER_QUERY

```
ALTER DATABASE [<Database Name>] SET QUERY_STORE ( MAX_PLANS_PER_QUERY =
<Value> );
```

WAIT_STATISTICS_CAPTURE_MODE

The WAIT_STATISTICS_CAPTURE_MODE default is ON. This setting is not available in SQL Server 2016. The only other option for this setting is OFF. Wait statistics are discussed more in Chapter 9. The T-SQL for configuring this setting is in Listing 3-13.

Listing 3-13. T-SQL to set WAIT_STATISTICS_CAPTURE_MODE

```
ALTER DATABASE [<Database Name>] SET QUERY_STORE ( WAIT_STATISTICS_CAPTURE_
MODE = <Value> );
```

Changing Configuration Using the GUI

By default, Query Store is turned off on-premise SQL Server databases and turned on by default in Azure SQL Database. To view the properties and change them, you would connect to your SQL Server instance, right-click on your database, and click on Properties. From there, click on the Query Store link on the left-hand side of the properties window. See Figure 3-1 to see example of what the properties windows looks like.

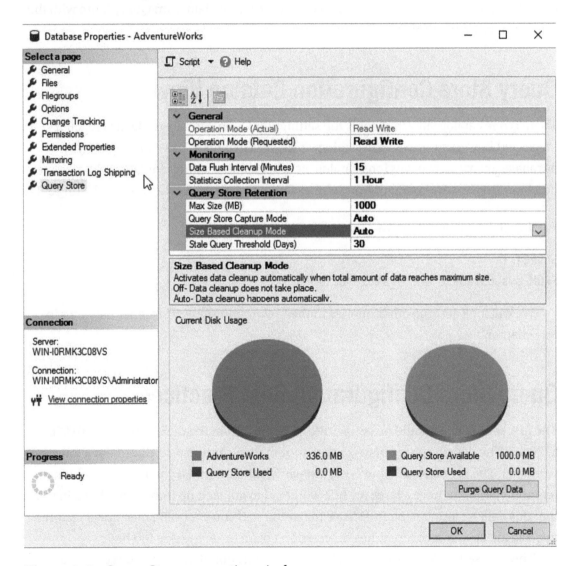

Figure 3-1. *Query Store properties window*

Note   You cannot change or see the `MAX_PLANS_PER_QUERY` or `WAIT_STATISTICS_CAPTURE_MODE` options in the GUI or the three options that come with the `CUSTOM QUERY_STORE_CAPTURE_MODE` setting.

You can see how much space the database is taking up and Query Store is taking up on the pie chart on the left. On the pie chart on the right, you can see the used and available space in Query Store. You also can purge all the data from Query Store with the Purge Query Data button.

Query Store Configuration Catalog View

There is one catalog view that holds the settings for Query Store: `sys.database_query_store_options`. For more on the catalog views, see Chapter 5. You can use the `sys.database_query_store_options` catalog view to view the settings for Query Store in the database. To view the configuration settings for Query Store, use the query in Listing 3-14.

Listing 3-14.   T-SQL to view Query Store Options

```
SELECT *
FROM sys.database_query_store_options
```

We will look at some other queries in the Maintaining Query Store section later in this chapter.

Query Store Configuration Best Practices

The first setting that should be configured differently than the default is `MAX_STORAGE_SIZE_MB`. The default setting here is much too small to capture a 30-day or even longer workload. The general guideline is to start with 2048 MBs and if you must keep a longer retention period or have a large ad-hoc workload to adjust it up from there. Keep in mind that this data is stored in the PRIMARY filegroup, so if you are doing piecemeal restores, this will affect your recovery times, so you don't want to set the size too high.

The next setting for on-premise SQL Servers that should be changed is `QUERY_STORE_CAPTURE_MODE`. This setting should be changed from `ALL` to `AUTO` unless you need to capture queries that take up insignificant resources or execute very few times. Capturing insignificant queries just causes more work for Query Store and takes more disk space in Query Store. So before leaving this setting to ALL, take those things into consideration.

The recommended setting for SIZE_BASED_CLEANUP_MODE is to leave the setting on AUTO because if the MAX_STORAGE_SIZE_MB is reached because it cannot clean up data, the OPERATION_MODE will be automatically switched to READ_ONLY mode leaving in a state where you are not collecting new data.

The next setting you may consider changing is INTERVAL_LENGTH_MINUTES. The recommended setting is the default of 60 unless you need data at a more granular level. In that case, going as low as 15 would be advisable as systems processing 60,000 transactions per second on the right hardware have been able to keep up aggregating that data. If you have more of an ad-hoc workload vs. stored procedure or parameterize workload, you are going to want to keep this setting higher as it will be writing more data.

The recommended setting for WAIT_STATISTICS_CAPTURE_MODE is ON because it gives more troubleshooting insight for your queries. Turning this setting OFF handicaps your ability to use a great feature built into Query Store for seeing what queries are causing which wait statistics to occur on your server by your database.

Parameterization and Query Store

We have touched on this topic a bit when talking about the QUERY_STORE_CAPTURE_MODE setting for query store. Let's explore what this means more. First let's discuss the difference between paramterize queries and ad-hoc queries. A parameterized query comes in as a stored procedure, function, trigger, or via sp_executesql. What makes it parameterized is that each variable that comes in has a predefined data type that SQL Server uses each time the query is called. For example, see the code in Listing 3-15 where we query for the LastName from a Customer table, but we have the data type fixed to 20 characters.

Listing 3-15. Stored Procedure Demonstrating a Parametrized Call to SQL Server

```
CREATE PROCEDURE dbo.GetName
      @LastName VARCHAR(20)
AS
SET NOCOUNT ON;

SELECT FirstName,
      LastName
```

```
FROM dbo.Customer
WHERE LastName = @LastName;
GO

EXEC dbo.GetName @LastName = 'Boggiano';
```

So, what this means is that every time this procedure is called it gets rolled up into one record per runtime interval in Query Store because it always has the variable defined as VARCHAR(20). Now with an ad-hoc query doing the same thing, see Listing 3-16.

Listing 3-16. T-SQL for Ad-hoc query

```
SELECT FirstName,
       LastName
FROM dbo.Customer
WHERE LastName = 'Boggiano';
```

When this query is compiled, it stores the variable for LastName as eight characters, but if you run the same query with the LastName as Smith, it will store the query with a variable as five characters giving you two records per runtime interval in Query Store. The data doesn't get aggregated and therefore makes it harder to tune and troubleshoot queries that are of the same type. Ad-hoc queries also bloat the size of Query Store due to the number of unique questions it must keep track of.

Impact of "Drop and Create" vs. "Alter"

Query Store stores the object_id of the procedures, triggers, and functions that execute inside of the database. By altering these objects, you preserve the object_id of the object; if you use the "drop and create" method, you will no longer have the same object_id so the data will no longer be aggregated together going forward. So, if you make a change to try to improve performance and you decide to go and compare the performance in Query Store to prior runtime intervals, you will not be able to view the results in the Query Store reports, you will have to query the catalog views. In SQL Server 2017, the syntax "CREATE OR ALTER" was introduced so you can avoid the need to code for a DROP/CREATE operation.

Impact of Database Renaming

Inside execution plans all objects are referenced as three-part names `database.schema.object` because you have the potential of doing cross-database queries. Renaming a database will cause plan forcing to fail, causing recompilation of all queries using those forced plans on each execution.

Reducing Recovery Times with Trace Flags

By default, all queries are blocked from running in the database until Query Store is loaded if Query Store is enabled on the database. This is where trace flag 7752 comes into play. By default, this behavior is on in Azure SQL Database, but on-premise you can turn on this trace flag and have Query Store load asynchronously, and in the background will be in a read-only state until it is completely loaded, so queries can process while Query Store loads, but you will not be capturing them. You can tell this is an issue on your system if you notice the wait stat `QDS_LOADDB` being high after a restart of your SQL Server instance. With this being the default behavior in Azure SQL Database it is quite possible it will become the default behavior in the on-premise product so we might want to go ahead and enable it now and get the benefits of faster startup times for our SQL Server instances. This also has the same effects on failovers.

Trace flag 7745 controls rather your SQL Server instance takes the time to flush all the Query Store data to disk while SQL Server instance is being shut down. This can take a considerable amount of time that you may not be willing to wait to depend on what you have your `DATA_FLUSH_INTERVAL_SECONDS` set to and/or the number of databases with Query Store enabled on your instance. The recommendation here would be to turn on this trace flag on because if you tell SQL Server to shut down; you don't want to wait for data to be flush to disk, you want to get your SQL Server instance back up and running as fast as possible.

Query Store and Memory-Optimized Tables

Memory-optimized tables are tables that are stored entirely in memory. Therefore, Query Store tracks a limited number of metrics when tracking queries that executed against memory-optimized tables because those tables are stored in memory. Query Store does not track I/O due to the table residing entirely in memory and query memory used. It does, however, track other metrics such as duration, CPU time, the degree of parallelism, and the row count. When viewing reports discussed in Chapter 4, keep this in mind if you use memory-optimized tables.

Configuring Query Store for Natively Compiled Stored Procedures

Similarly, to memory-optimized tables, natively compiled stored procedures are treated differently by Query Store. Query plans and query text are stored in Query Store by default for natively compiled stored procedure and a flag denotes these procedures in the catalog view sys.query_store_plan. However, runtime statistics are not stored in the sys.query_store_runtime_stats catalog view by default. To capture runtime statistics, you must use the procedure sys.sp_xtp_control_query_exec_stats. The procedure can be used to capture statistics for all natively compiled procedures at the instance level or just particular ones you need to troubleshoot. There is a performance overhead associated with collecting these statistics. Listing 3-17 shows you how to set up a natively compiled stored procedure to capture runtime statistics.

Listing 3-17. Setup Query Store to capture runtime statistics for a natively compiled stored procedure

```
DECLARE @dbid INT = DB_ID('<database>');
DECLARE @object_id INT = OBJECT_ID('<InMemoryProcedure>');

EXEC sys.sp_xtp_control_query_exec_stats
  @new_collection_value = 1,
  @database_id = @dbid,
  @xtp_object_id = @object_id;
```

Listing 3-18 shows you how to capture statistics for all natively compiled stored procedures on an instance.

Listing 3-18. Setup Query Store to capture runtime statistics for all natively compiled stored procedures on the instance

```
EXEC sys.sp_xtp_control_query_exec_stats
    @new_collection_value = 1;
```

To turn off the collection of statistics, run the same code in Listings 3-16 or 3-17 and change the parameter @new_collection_value to 0.

> **Note**   These settings are reset to not capture statistics on the event that the SQL Server instance is shut down or restarted. If you need it to persist in collecting statistics, you will need to set up a startup stored procedure or a SQL Agent job that runs at startup.

Enabling and Disabling Automatic Plan Regression Correction (APRC)

To enable automatic plan regression correction (APRC), you can run the following code in Listing 3-19 for one database or the code in Listing 3-20 to enable Query Store on all databases where query store is enabled and is a READ_WRITE state. What is APRC and how it works is discussed more in Chapter 9.

Listing 3-19. T-SQL to enable APRC

```
ALTER DATABASE [<Database>]
     SET AUTOMATIC_TUNING ( FORCE_LAST_GOOD_PLAN = ON );
```

Listing 3-20. T-SQL to enable APRC where database is online and Query Store is enabled

```
DECLARE @SQL NVARCHAR(MAX) = N''

SELECT @SQL += REPLACE(N'ALTER DATABASE [{{DBNAME}}] SET AUTOMATIC_TUNING (
FORCE_LAST_GOOD_PLAN = ON ',
     '{{DBName}}', [name])
FROM sys.databases
WHERE state_desc = 'ONLINE'
     AND is_query_store_on = 1
ORDER BY [name];

EXEC (@SQL);;
```

To turn off Query Store, we run the same queries with OFF instead on as seen in code listings above as seen in Listings 3-21 and 3-22.

Listing 3-21. T-SQL to disable APRC

```
ALTER DATABASE [<Database>]
    SET AUTOMATIC_TUNING ( FORCE_LAST_GOOD_PLAN = OFF );
```

Listing 3-22. T-SQL to disable APRC where database is online and Query Store is enabled

```
DECLARE @SQL NVARCHAR(MAX) = N'';

SELECT @SQL += REPLACE(N'ALTER DATABASE [{{DBNAME}}] SET AUTOMATIC_TUNING (
FORCE_LAST_GOOD_PLAN = OFF ',
    '{{DBName}}', [name])
FROM sys.databases
WHERE state_desc = 'ONLINE'
    AND is_query_store_on = 1
ORDER BY [name];

EXEC (@SQL);
```

Maintaining Query Store

After you have Query Store configured, there are some items you may need to keep an eye out for. Sometimes the state of Query Store will change from READ_WRITE to READ_ONLY or ERROR and you will need to know when this happends and correct this. You also need to monitor the space usage to determine if you are capturing the write amount of data for the period of time you need and to make sure you don't run out of space. You also need to know if any plans you forced are failing and how to track those. You may also need to remove plans and queries from Query Store. Finally, you may need to reset the wait statistics.

Monitoring Desired vs. Actual State

First, to maintain Query Store, you will want to make sure the desired_state and the actual_state of Query Store match. You can run the code in Listing 3-23 to check in single database or the code in Listing 3-24 to check all the databases in Query Store enabled on your instance.

Listing 3-23. T-SQL to check Query Store's desired state vs. actual state

```
SELECT DB_NAME() database_name,
      actual_state_desc,
      desired_state_desc
FROM sys.database_query_store_options
WHERE desired_state_desc <> actual_state_desc
```

Listing 3-24. T-SQL to check Query Store's desired state vs. actual state on all databases

```
DECLARE @SQL NVARCHAR(MAX) = N'';

SELECT @SQL += REPLACE(REPLACE(N'USE [{{DBName}}];
        SELECT
              "{{DBName}}" database_name,
              actual_state_desc,
              desired_state_desc
        FROM {{DBName}}.sys.database_query_store_options
        WHERE desired_state_desc <> actual_state_desc '
    ,'{{DBName}}', [name])
    ,'"', "")
FROM sys.databases
WHERE is_query_store_on = 1
ORDER BY [name];

EXEC (@SQL);
```

Query Store Read-Only States

Query Store can enter the READ_ONLY state from READ_WRITE without telling for a number of reasons. The reason is stored in the readonly_reason as a bit map in the sys.query_store_options catalog view. In Table 3-2 you will find a list of the reasons.

Table 3-2. *Query Store read-only state reasons*

readonly_reason bit map	Description
1	Database is in read-only mode
2	Database is in single-user mode
4	Database is in emergency mode
8	Database is a secondary replica (Always On and Azure SQL Database geo-replication)
65536	Reached limit set by MAX_STORAGE_SIZE_MB
131072	The number of different statements has reached memory limit. In this case you should consider remove queries from the Query Store or upgrading service tier Applies to Azure SQL Database
262144	In-memory size limit has been hit. Items will be persisted to disk until space is freed up in memory. Query Store will be temporarily in read-only mode Applies to Azure SQL Database
524288	Database has reached disk size limit so Query Store can no longer grow Applies to Azure SQL Database

How to Fix Query Store in Error State

Starting in SQL Server 2017, Query Store can enter an error state. This can cause potential performance problems when you depend on manual plan forcing or auto plan regression correction. This is a rare race condition that can occur without you knowing. The recommended fix is to first try to turn OFF Query Store and place it in READ_WRITE mode. If that doesn't work, the persisted data is corrupted on disk, so we run sys.sp_query_store_consistency_check. Finally, clear Query Store of all data.

In Listing 3-25 you have code to run against all the databases with Query Store in ERROR state to fix the ERROR state.

Listing 3-25. T-SQL to fix error state on all databases on instance

```
DECLARE @SQL AS NVARCHAR(MAX) = N'';

SELECT @SQL += REPLACE(N'USE [{{DBName}}]
    --Try Changing to READ_WRITE
    IF EXISTS (SELECT * FROM sys.database_query_store_options
        WHERE actual_state=3)
    BEGIN
        BEGIN TRY
            ALTER DATABASE [{{DBName}}] SET QUERY_STORE =
                OFF
            ALTER DATABASE [{{DBName}}] SET QUERY_STORE =
                READ_WRITE
        END TRY
        BEGIN CATCH
        SELECT
            ERROR_NUMBER() AS ErrorNumber
            ,ERROR_SEVERITY() AS ErrorSeverity
            ,ERROR_STATE() AS ErrorState
            ,ERROR_PROCEDURE() AS ErrorProcedure
            ,ERROR_LINE() AS ErrorLine
            ,ERROR_MESSAGE() AS ErrorMessage;
        END CATCH;
    END

    --Run sys.sp_query_store_consistency_check
    IF EXISTS (SELECT * FROM sys.database_query_store_options
        WHERE actual_state=3)
    BEGIN
        BEGIN TRY
            EXEC
    [{{DBName}}].sys.sp_query_store_consistency_check
            ALTER DATABASE [{{DBName}}] SET QUERY_STORE =
```

```
                        ON
                ALTER DATABASE [{{DBName}}] SET QUERY_STORE
                    (OPERATION_MODE = READ_WRITE)
        END TRY
        BEGIN CATCH
        SELECT
                ERROR_NUMBER() AS ErrorNumber
                ,ERROR_SEVERITY() AS ErrorSeverity
                ,ERROR_STATE() AS ErrorState
                ,ERROR_PROCEDURE() AS ErrorProcedure
                ,ERROR_LINE() AS ErrorLine
                ,ERROR_MESSAGE() AS ErrorMessage;
        END CATCH;
    END

    --Run purge Query Store
    IF EXISTS (SELECT * FROM sys.database_query_store_options
        WHERE actual_state=3)
    BEGIN
        BEGIN TRY
                ALTER DATABASE [{{DBName}}] SET QUERY_STORE
                    CLEAR
                ALTER DATABASE [{{DBName}}] SET QUERY_STORE
                    (OPERATION_MODE = READ_WRITE)
        END TRY
        BEGIN CATCH
        SELECT
                ERROR_NUMBER() AS ErrorNumber
                ,ERROR_SEVERITY() AS ErrorSeverity
                ,ERROR_STATE() AS ErrorState
                ,ERROR_PROCEDURE() AS ErrorProcedure
                ,ERROR_LINE() AS ErrorLine
                ,ERROR_MESSAGE() AS ErrorMessage
        END CATCH;
    END
```

```
        ,'{{DBName}}', [name])
FROM sys.databases
WHERE is_query_store_on = 1;

EXEC (@SQL);
```

Tip   Due to the potential performance, impact recommendation would set the above code as a SQL Agent job to run a regular basis so you don't get caught off guard when the Query Store is in an ERROR state.

Monitoring Space Usage

If you do set the CLEANUP_POLICY to AUTO as discussed earlier in the chapter, you will need to monitor the space usage yourself to make sure Query Store doesn't switch to read-only mode. By default, Query Store will, at 90% capacity, clean up to an 80% capacity. If you have the MAX_STORAGE_SIZE_MB size set too low and have a large amount of transactions coming through, it is possible for Query Store to grow bigger than the max size specified. In Listing 3-26, you will find code to monitor space for a single database on your instance that is at 90% capacity.

Listing 3-26.   T-SQL code to check if Query Store is at 90% capacity

```
USE [<Database>];
GO

SELECT current_storage_size_mb,
     max_storage_size_mb,
FROM sys.database_query_store_options
WHERE CAST(CAST(current_storage_size_mb AS
     DECIMAL(21, 2)) / CAST(max_storage_size_mb AS
     DECIMAL(21, 2)) * 100 AS DECIMAL(4, 2)) >= 90
     AND size_based_cleanup_mode_desc = 'OFF';
```

Tip   You will want to put this code in a SQL Agent Job and add code to email you to alert when Query Store is near capacity, so that you may address it.

How to Clear Query Store

You may find it necessary to clear the data manually from Query Store. You may use one of the following two methods in Listings 3-27 and 3-28 to this.

Listing 3-27. T-SQL to clear all the data out of Query Store

```
ALTER DATABASE [<Database Name>] SET QUERY_STORE CLEAR ALL;
```

Listing 3-28. Stored procedure to clear all the data out of Query Store

```
USE [<Database>];
GO

EXEC sys.sp_query_store_flush_db;
```

Failed Plan Forcing

Plan forcing can fail for a number of reasons such as an index in the plan being changed or dropped, online index rebuilds while trying to write to the index, or a hint conflict. It's important to track failed plans so you know if you are getting the performance gain you expected when you forced the plans. There are two ways to track forced plans. The first is with T-SQL. You can query the catalog view sys.query_store_plan to see the last failure reason and failed count as seen in Listing 3-29.

Listing 3-29. Query of plans with failed forced plans

```
SELECT plan_id,
       force_failure_count,
       last_force_failure_reason
FROM sys.query_store_plan
```

Because the above method only shows the last forced plan reason then increments a counter and is per database, you may want to set up an extended events session that can track failed plan forcing across your SQL Server instance and set up a SQL Agent job to query and send out alerts. In Listing 3-30 you will find an extended events session that can set up to capture failed plan forcing.

Listing 3-30. Extended events session to capture failing force plans

```
CREATE EVENT SESSION [QueryStore_Forcing_Plan_Failure]
      ON SERVER
ADD EVENT qds.query_store_plan_forcing_failed
ADD TARGET package0.ring_buffer WITH
  (
  MAX_MEMORY=4096 KB,
  EVENT_RETENTION_MODE=ALLOW_SINGLE_EVENT_LOSS,
  MAX_DISPATCH_LATENCY=30 SECONDS,
  MAX_EVENT_SIZE=0 KB,
  MEMORY_PARTITION_MODE=NONE,
  TRACK_CAUSALITY=OFF,
  STARTUP_STATE=ON
);
```

Removing Plans and Queries

There are times when you may want to remove a plan from Query Store. You can use the procedure sys.sp_query_store_remove_plan to remove any plan from Query Store. When you run the procedure, it also removes the runtime statistics associated with that plan. It requires the EXECUTE permission on the database and DELETE permission on the Query Store catalog views. See Listing 3-31 for an example of how to remove a plan from Query Store.

Listing 3-31. Stored procedure to remove a query from the Query Store

```
EXECUTE sys.sp_query_store_remove_plan @plan_id = <plan_id>;
```

Similarly, there are times when you may want to remove a query from Query Store, such as when you have several ad-hoc queries taking up space in Query Store. You can use the procedure sys.sp_query_store_remove_query to remove any query from Query Store. When you run the procedure, it also removes the runtime statistics. It requires the EXECUTE permission on the database and DELETE permission on the Query Store catalog views. See Listing 3-32 for an example of how to remove a query from Query Store by filling in the query_id.

Listing 3-32. Stored procedure to remove a query from the query store

```
EXECUTE sys.sp_query_store_remove_query @query_id = <query_id>;
```

Reset Statistics for a Plan

The stored procedure sys.sp_query_store_reset_exec_stats clears runtime statistics for a given plan but leaves the plan in Query Store. It requires the EXECUTE permission on the database and DELETE permission on the Query Store catalog views. See Listing 3-33 for an example of how to reset statistics for a plan from Query Store by filling in the plan_id.

Listing 3-33. Query to reset statistics for a plan

```
USE [<Database>];
GO

EXECUTE sys.sp_query_store_reset_exec_stats @plan_id = <plan_id>;
```

Conclusion

In this chapter we have learned about all the configuration options for Query Store and the recommended settings. We talked about the effect of having parameterized queries on Query Store vs. ad-hoc queries. Then we talked about the impact of using the drop and create process for stored procedures, functions, and triggers on seeing statistics for those objects. We talked about how to reduce the shutdown and startup times of the SQL Server instance by using trace flags. We covered how to capture data for natively compiled stored procedures. Finally, we discussed various methods to maintain Query Store.

CHAPTER 4

Standard Query Store Reports

SQL Server Management Studio (SSMS) has seven built-in reports for Query Store. These reports give us the ability to quickly view performance data and troubleshoot performance issues in a graphical interface and transition the data into a grid view. In this chapter, we will explore how to interact with these reports and how they complement each other and work together. A list of the reports can be found below the database in Object Explorer as seen in Figure 4-1:

Figure 4-1. *Object Explorer view of reports for Query Store*

T. Boggiano and G. Fritchey, *Query Store for SQL Server 2019*, https://doi.org/10.1007/978-1-4842-5004-4_4

Regressed Queries Report

The first report we will look at is the Regressed Queries report. This report displays information on which queries over the specified period have started degrading in performance. There are several things you can do to navigate around inside of these reports, but first let's take a glance at this report in Figure 4-2.

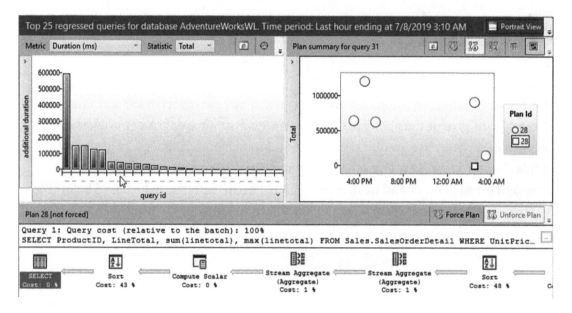

Figure 4-2. *Regressed Queries report*

Each bar on the left-hand side represents a different query that could be part of a stored procedure, trigger, user-defined function or be an ad-hoc query that executed in the specified period of time. The default period of time for the report is the last hour. If you click on any of the bars, the query plan will change at the bottom to show the estimated plan for that query. If you hover over any of the bars, it will show you stats for each one of the queries the bar represents as seen in Figure 4-3.

Query Id	31
Object Id	1799677459
Object Name	p_sel_get_sales_rollup_by_product_linetotal
Additional Duration (ms)	146688.21
Total Duration (ms) Recent	1061720.28
Total Duration (ms) History	3530137.65
Execution Count Recent	359
Execution Count History	1385
Plan Count	1

(@i int)SELECT ProductID, LineTotal, sum(linetotal), max(linetotal)
        FROM Sales.SalesOrderDetail
        WHERE UnitPrice < @i
        group by rollup(productid, linetotal)
        ORDER BY ProductID, LineTotal

Figure 4-3. *Regressed Queries report hover over bar statistics*

On the left-hand side on the top left-hand pane, you can control the type of regression that is shown to you by clicking the bar that defaults to additional duration. Other options are seen in Figure 4-4:

additional duration
total duration recent
total duration history
execution count recent
execution count history
plan count

Figure 4-4. *Additional options for types of regressions*

In the bottom pane on any report that shows you a query plan, you will see a box with three dots in the upper right-hand corner; once you click on the box, it will take the query text and put in a Query Editor window as seen in Figure 4-5.

Figure 4-5. *Button to open query test in a Query Editor window*

Also, on the bottom pane, you have two buttons as seen in Figure 4-6 that allow to force and unforce plans based on which plan you have highlighted and shown in the pane.

Figure 4-6. *Regressed Queries report force and unforce plan buttons*

You will also see the estimated plan that the stored procedure, function, trigger, or ad-hoc query generated during the period of time of the reporting period. Similarly, as you run an estimated or actual plan in a Query Editor window of SQL Server Management Studio (SSMS), you can hover over each plan operator to see detail statistics, warnings, and the percentages of where the most work has taken place. You can right-click on the plan to get the same options to as you get in the Query Editor window in SSMS as seen in Figure 4-7.

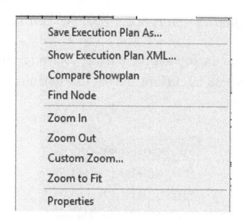

Figure 4-7. *Regressed Queries report plan options*

Note   The bottom pane functions the same way across all reports that show query plans.

Overall Resource Consumption Report

The Overall Resource Consumption report shows the resources the database is consuming by default for the last month. The report defaults to showing four categories of performance in total amounts: duration in milliseconds, execution count, CPU time in milliseconds, and logical reads in kilobytes. Here is an example of a report shown in Figure 4-8:

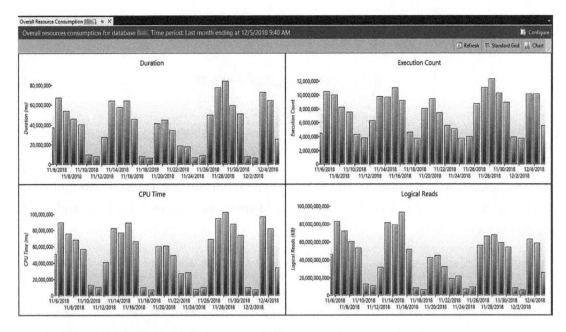

Figure 4-8. *Overall Resource Consumption report*

If you double-click on any of the bars shown in the chart, you will automatically open the next report we will be talking about, the Top Resource Consuming Queries report. If you hover over any of the bars, you will get a list of statistics for the period of time for the bar as seen in Figure 4-9.

Interval Start	2019-07-08 02:59:00.000 -07:00
Interval End	2019-07-08 03:00:00.000 -07:00
Execution Count	17551
Duration (ms)	10661460.16
CPU Time (ms)	2143751.88
Logical Reads (KB)	759776992
Logical Writes (KB)	2680152
Physical Reads (KB)	9985784
CLR Time (ms)	103.36
DOP	17551
Memory Consumption (KB)	51032040
Row Count	147447592
Log Memory Used (KB)	70631.19
Temp DB Memory Used (KB)	7951104
Wait Time (ms)	1415944

Figure 4-9. *Overall Consumption Report hover statistics*

In the top right-hand corner, you have four buttons that allow you to control the reports. You can see a close-up picture of these in Figure 4-10:

Figure 4-10. *Overall Resource Consumption report buttons*

The Refresh button will allow you to refresh the report on the screen. The Standard Grid button allows you to view the data in a grid view; see Figures 4-11, 4-12, and 4-13 for an example.

	total execution count	total duration	total cpu time	total logical reads	total logical writes	total physical reads
1	5	10.27	10.26	680	0	0
2	39	255.26	75	6816	0	0
3	16	41.74	26.12	2176	0	0
4	22	58.02	39.12	2992	0	0
5	48	307.93	93.69	6528	0	0

Figure 4-11. *Overall Resource Consumption report standard grid view*

total clr time	total dop	total memory consumption	total row count	total log memory used	total temp db memory used
0	5	5280	60	0	0
0	39	40128	1140	13.5	0
0	16	16896	272	0	0
0	22	23232	616	0	0
0	48	50688	726	0	0

Figure 4-12. *Overall Resource Consumption report standard grid view*

total wait time	interval start	interval end
8567993	2019-07-08 02:52:00.000 -07:00	2019-07-08 02:53:00.000 -07:00
1415944	2019-07-08 02:54:00.000 -07:00	2019-07-08 02:55:00.000 -07:00
8567993	2019-07-08 02:56:00.000 -07:00	2019-07-08 02:57:00.000 -07:00
1415944	2019-07-08 02:57:00.000 -07:00	2019-07-08 02:58:00.000 -07:00
8567993	2019-07-08 02:58:00.000 -07:00	2019-07-08 02:59:00.000 -07:00

Figure 4-13. *Overall Resource Consumption report standard grid view*

The Standard Grid view contains a lot more columns than you get in the Standard View with charts. You can click on the column headings of any of the columns, and it will sort the columns and place an arrow showing which way it sorted the data. By default, it is sorted by the interval start date and time.

The Chart button allows you to switch back to the Chart View if you are in the Standard Grid View.

Finally, the Configure button allows you to control items on the Chart View and the Time Interval shown in either the Standard View or the Chart View. Figure 4-14 shows the options available under the Configure button.

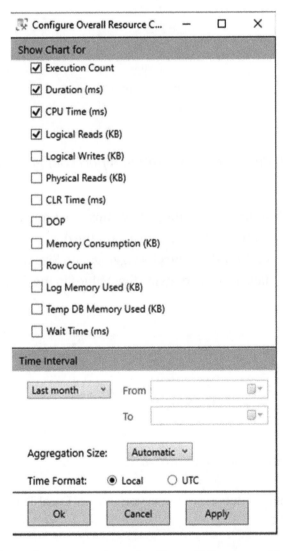

Figure 4-14. *Configure button options for Overall Resource Consumption reports*

On the top half of the screen as of SSMS, Figure 4-14 shows you all the metrics that are available to be displayed in the Chart View. You can also use it to remove any item from the view.

The bottom half of the screen in Figure 4-14 applies to both the Chart View and Standard Grid View. You can change the Time Interval from the last month which is the default to a value seen in Figure 4-15 to view a different period of time.

Figure 4-15. *Overall Resource Consumption report configure time interval drop-down*

When you select Custom from the drop-down box, the From and To boxes will no longer be greyed and out and you will be able to edit the days by typing or selecting from a calendar. Next, there is a drop-down box for Aggregation Size where you can specify the intervals it rolls the data into for your viewing. Values in the drop-down are shown in Figure 4-16.

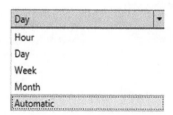

Figure 4-16. *Aggregation Size drop-down*

Finally, you can select if data is shown to you in your Local Time Zone time or UTC zone.

Tip   This is the best report for validating whether or not your system is meeting your expected baselines you have established and for seeing if something unusual is happening on the server.

Top Resource Consuming Queries Report

The Top Resource Consuming Queries Report by default shows the top 25 queries summed up by total duration for the last hour. In Figure 4-17, you can see an example of what this report looks like. Like the other reports we have discussed, there are many options we can look at the top of the report.

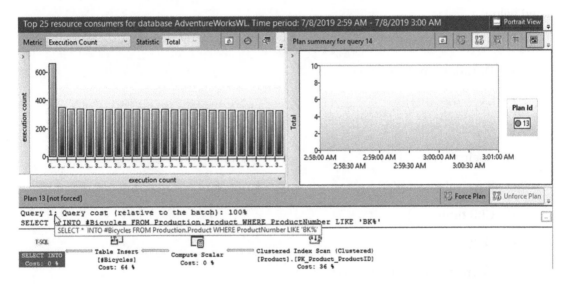

Figure 4-17.   *Top Consuming Resources report*

At the top right-hand corner, we have three buttons that control the overall reports as seen in Figure 4-18. The Portrait View button will move the three separate panes stack on top of each other instead of having the two panes beside each other at the top and one on the bottom. The Configure button does the same as we have seen in the last report; refer to Figure 4-14.

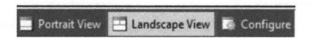

Figure 4-18. *Top Consuming Resources report buttons*

When we look at Figure 4-19, we can see the following buttons to allow you to control the top left-hand corner of the screen.

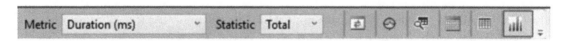

Figure 4-19. *Top Consuming Resource report option bar*

First, we have the metric we want to see for the top 25 queries by in the drop-down listed below:

- Execution count

- Duration (ms) (default)

- CPU time (ms)

- Logical reads (KB)

- Logical writes (KB)

- Physical reads (KB)

- CLR time (ms)

- DOP

- Memory consumption (KB)

- Row count

- Log memory used (KB)

- Tempdb memory usage (KB)

- Wait time (ms)

Then instead of having the statistics by total, you can change the statistics to the following values:

- Avg

- Max

- Min

- Std dev

- Total (default)

The Refresh button will refresh the report to the current period of time specified. Next, you have a button that will let you jump to the Track Queries Report to look at the query highlighted. The button with magnifying glass takes the selected query's text and pops it a new query window for you to view. The Grid View button will provide you with additional metrics to look for each query. See Figures 4-20, 4-21, 4-22, and 4-23 for an example of what the Grid View looks like.

	query id	object id	object name	query sql text	total duration	total cpu time
1	24	1687677060	p_sel_produ...	(@i int)SELEC...	97816.87	18532.68
2	51	1431676148	p_sel_produ...	(@i int)SELEC...	236.04	165.43
3	54	1415676091	p_sel_produ...	(@i int)SELEC...	202.84	156.63
4	1	1607676775	p_sel_empl...	(@i int,@prod...	58.56	40.8
5	4	1607676775	p_sel_empl...	(@productNu...	4652.02	1206.26

Figure 4-20. *Top Consuming Resources additional grid view*

	total logical reads	total logical writes	total physical reads	total clr time	total dop
1	3514368	0	0	0	352
2	40440	0	0	0	337
3	40440	0	0	0	337
4	5344	0	0	0	334
5	76824	0	0	14.14	334

Figure 4-21. *Top Consuming Resources additional grid view*

	total memory consumption	total row count	total log memory used	total temp db memory used
1	568832	4445	0	0
2	345088	13029	0	0
3	345088	13984	0	0
4	0	334	0	0
5	662656	950	0	0

Figure 4-22. *Top Consuming Resources additional grid view*

	total wait time	▼ execution count	plan count
1	89610.91	352	1
2	73.47	337	1
3	44.1	337	1
4	17.28	334	1
5	4265.4	334	1

Figure 4-23. *Top Consuming Resources additional grid view*

Columns will vary in this view based on the statistic you choose to look at; for example, the figure is based on totals, but if you pick avg, the view will show averages. The columns in general that are included in figures above are as follows :

- Query_id
- Object_id
- Object_name
- Query_sql_text
- Duration
- CPU time
- Logical reads
- Logical writes
- Physical reads
- CLR time
- DOP

- Memory consumption

- Row count

- Log memory used

- Temp db memory used

- Wait time

- Execution count

- Plan count

The Regular Grid View button shows far fewer columns as seen in Figure 4-24. The Regular Grid View concentrates on the metric and statistic you are looking at in the chart rather than showing all the metrics. Note both views have the ability for you to change which metric and statistic you want to view the data inside the view without returning to the Chart View.

Top 25 resource consumers for database AdventureWorks2017. Time period: Last hour ending							
Metric Duration (ms)		Statistic Total					
	query id	object id	object name	query sql text	▼ total duration	execution count	plan count
1	54	1815677516	p_sel_get_s...	(@i int)SELEC...	3329030.84	308	1
2	4	1479676319	p_sel_disco...	SELECT p.Na...	1142454.79	355	1
3	12	1495676376	p_calc_reve...	SELECT 'Total ...	1130718.69	355	1
4	10	1831677573	p_sel_prod_...	SELECT p.Na...	1059439.26	332	1
5	29	1799677459	p_sel_get_s...	(@i int)SELEC...	488452.74	311	1
6	48	1623676832	p_sel_grou...	SELECT Produ...	45943.4	328	1
7	39	1591676718	p_sel_total_...	SELECT Sales...	38858.22	358	1
8	25	1735677231	p_sel_prod...	SELECT Produ...	38268.68	312	1
9	24	1767677345	p_sel_sales_...	(@i int)SELEC...	38216.17	315	1
10	57	1751677288	p_sel_prod...	SELECT Produ...	35573.38	303	1

Figure 4-24. *Top Consuming Resources regular grid view*

The Chart View button allows you to return to Chart View if you have entered either of the Grid Views.

You can change what is shown on the y-axis and x-axis of the chart on the Chart View on the pane as well. For the x-axis you have the options available in Figure 4-25, and for the y-axis you have the options available in Figure 4-26.

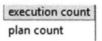

Figure 4-25. *Top Consuming Resources chart view y-axis options*

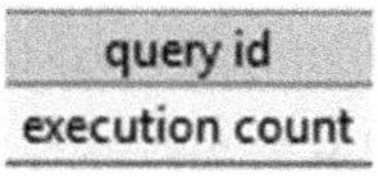

query id
execution count

Figure 4-26. *Top Consuming Resources chart view x-axis options*

The right-hand side of the screen shows you the plans and their IDs associated with each query; as you click on the query, this side of the screen adjusts along with the query plan shown at the bottom of the screen.

Also, in the first pane, if you hover over any of the bars for the queries, it will show you details about the query and the plan you currently have selected as seen in Figure 4-27.

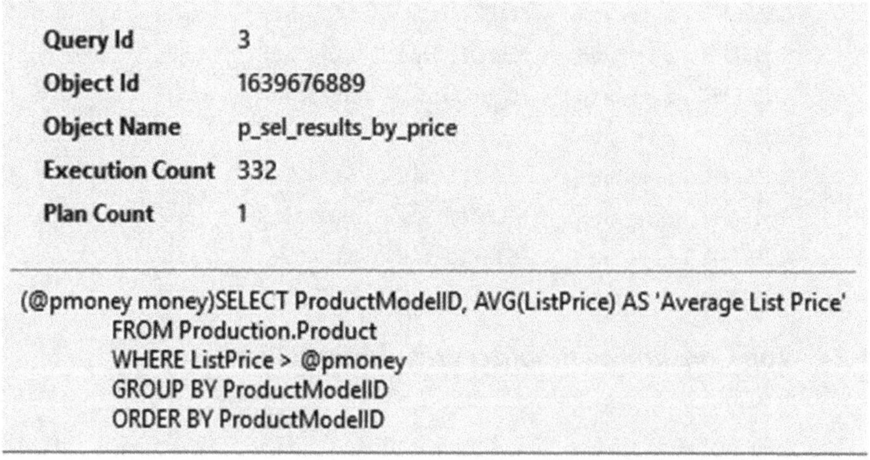

Query Id	3
Object Id	1639676889
Object Name	p_sel_results_by_price
Execution Count	332
Plan Count	1

```
(@pmoney money)SELECT ProductModelID, AVG(ListPrice) AS 'Average List Price'
        FROM Production.Product
        WHERE ListPrice > @pmoney
        GROUP BY ProductModelID
        ORDER BY ProductModelID
```

Figure 4-27. *Top Consuming Resources report query ID data*

On the left-hand side of the left-hand pane, you can change how you group the data. You can use whichever metric you selected from the top drop-down (duration, CPU, logical reads, etc.), execution count, and plan count as seen in Figure 4-28. The most useful here is plan count so you can find queries that have multiple plans which will help you identify possible queries with plans that can be forced.

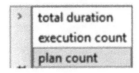

Figure 4-28. *Top Consuming Resources report left-hand pane group by drop-down*

On the left-hand pane in Portrait mode, there are a series of buttons that control what you may do with the plans being displayed for the selected query. Figure 4-29 shows you the buttons as we go through and explain what each one does.

Figure 4-29. *Top Consuming Resources report right-hand pane buttons*

You are already familiar with the Refresh button as it just refreshes the current report you are in. The next button forces the plan whichever plan is highlighted in the pane. The next button either tells you the plan is not forced or will unforce a plan if it has been forced previously. The next button will allow you to compare two plans if you click two of the dots in the pane below and hold the Ctrl key. Figure 4-30 shows an example of what comparing a plan looks like. The differences in the plan operators are highlighted in red in the plan diagram. Beside that, you will have what you see in Figure 4-31 which shows you more details about the differences in where the time is spent on each operation.

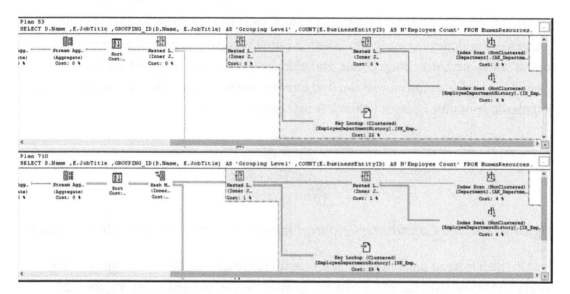

Figure 4-30. *Top Consuming Resources report comparing plan operator differences*

The differences seen in Figure 4-31 have a not equal sign highlighted in yellow.

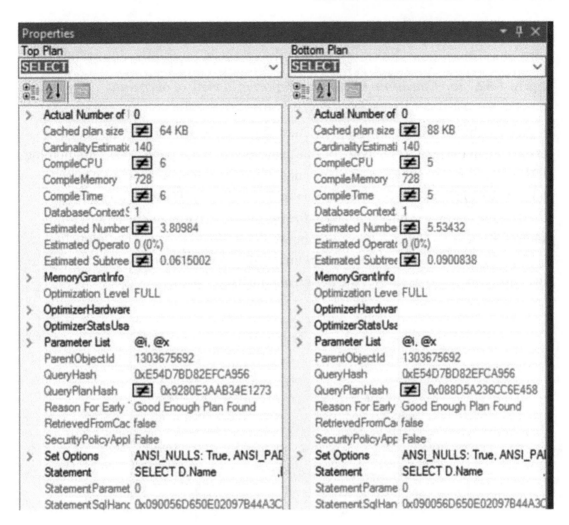

Figure 4-31. *Top Consuming Resources report comparing report details*

The next button shows you data for the plans in the Grid View as seen in Figure 4-32. The final button returns the pane into the Chart View.

	plan id	plan forced	execution type	execution count	min duration	max duration	avg duration	std dev duration	variation duration	last duration	▼ total duration	first execution time	last execution time
1	53	0	0	1186	0.16	7.62	0.45	0.42	0.93	482	9636.37	2018-12-10 11:00:28.3000000 +00:00	2018-12-10 12:49:20.0330000 +00:00
2	710	0	0	4	1.01	3.25	1.88	0.84	0.45	1519	37.59	2018-12-10 12:45:58.4570000 +00:00	2018-12-10 12:47:33.1270000 +00:00

Figure 4-32. *Top Consuming Resources report grid view of plan data*

In the right-hand pane, when it is in Chart View, you can hover over the plan and get data about the plan. Three types of icons will appear in this pane. A dot with nothing inside of it represents an unforced plan, a dot with a check mark represents a forced plan, and a square represents a failed execution of the query. These metrics change based on the metric you have selected at the top left-hand corner of the report; for example, if you have CPU Time chosen, you would see CPU instead of Duration. In Figure 4-33 you can see what the statistics an example of the statistics shown when you hover over a icon in the pane for the period of time it represents.

Plan Id	53
Execution Type	Completed
Plan Forced	No
Interval Start	2018-12-10 12:47:00.000 +00:00
Interval End	2018-12-10 12:48:00.000 +00:00
Execution Count	470
Total Duration (ms)	212.87
Avg Duration (ms)	0.45
Min Duration (ms)	0.16
Max Duration (ms)	7.62
Std Dev Duration (ms)	0.47
Variation Duration (ms)	1.04

Figure 4-33. *Top Consuming Resources report hover over query plan details*

Queries with Forced Plan Report

The Queries with Forced Plans report shows you the query plans that have been forced on your database. This report can be used to check back to make sure you still see the same performance improvement when you forced the plan or to see what plans have been forced on the database. A sample report can be seen in Figure 4-34:

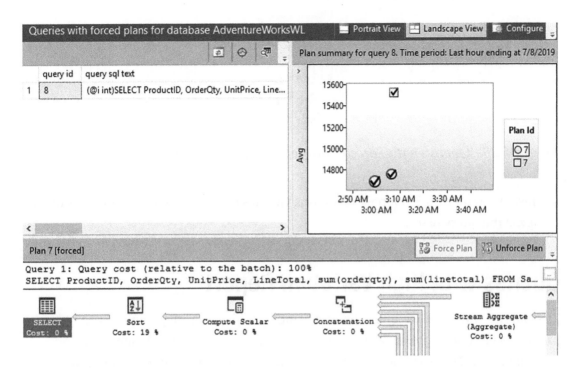

Figure 4-34. *Queries with Forced Plan report*

There are not as many configuration options in this report, but let's explore the buttons we do have available to us. The three buttons in the left-hand pane are familiar to us; the first is the refresh button. The second is to open this query in the Track Queries report. The last is to open the query text in the Query Editor window.

The right-hand pane has at the very top the same buttons from the Top Resource Consuming Queries report. One is to put the report in Landscape mode which stacks the panes. Another one is to change it back to its default Portrait mode. Then we have the Configure button which looks the same as the one in the Top Resource Consuming report in Figure 4-34. Underneath that, you have the Refresh button for the right-hand pane. There is a button to force a plan and a button to unforce a plan. Lastly is the button to compare plans.

In the bottom pane, you have the plan showed for the highlighted plan ID from the top right-hand pane and the buttons to force or unforce the plan selected as seen in Figure 4-34. On the left-hand side of the chart, you have the option to change the statistic that is used to display the dots which is defaulted to average; see Figure 4-35 for the other options.

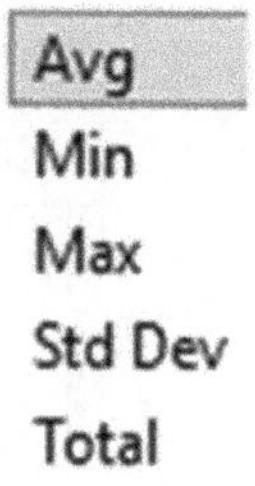

Avg
Min
Max
Std Dev
Total

Figure 4-35. *Queries with Forced Plan report y-axis options*

Just like in the Top Resource Consuming Queries report, you have the same options to look at the query plans.

Queries with High Variation Report

The Queries with High Variation report can indicate queries with parameterization problems. Parameterization occurs with a query that is executed with one value and is parameterized with a parameter then executed again with the different value and a different plan would be more appropriate due to data distribution. For example, if you were to execute a query looking for every living in Montana (MO), it would produce a plan searching based on statistics for a small data set than say if you search for everyone living in California (CA). An example of Queries with High Variation report is shown in Figure 4-36.

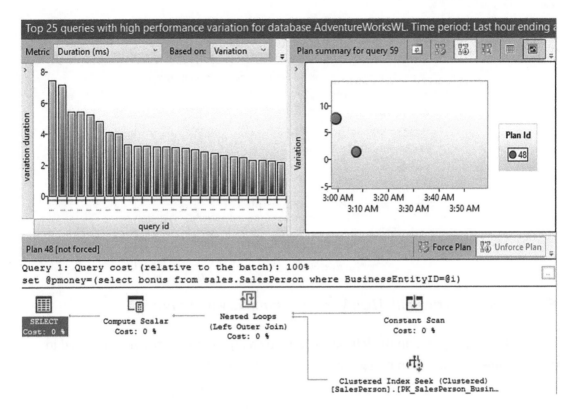

Figure 4-36. *High Variation report*

The few differences in this report with the Top Resource Consuming Queries Report are that under the Statistics drop-down, you only have two options: Variation and Standard Deviation, and there is no Configure button. When you hover over the bars, you receive more limited information as it only shows Variation and Standard Deviation for the metric you have selected as seen in Figure 4-37.

Query Id	33
Object Id	1319675749
Object Name	p_sel_get_originization_by_employee
Std Dev Duration (ms)	1.78
Avg Duration (ms)	0.33
Variation Duration (ms)	5.44
Execution Count	382
Plan Count	1

(@i int,@CurrentEmployee sys.hierarchyid)SELECT
@CurrentEmployee=OrganizationNode
from
HumanResources.Employee
where
BusinessEntityID=@i

Figure 4-37. *Queries with High Variation summary information*

You have the option on the left-hand pane to change the statistics that are used to display values; options can be seen in Figures 4-38 and 4-39.

std dev duration
avg duration
variation duration
execution count
plan count

Figure 4-38. *Queries with High Variation y-axis options*

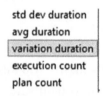

query id
query id
std dev duration
avg duration
variation duration
execution count

Figure 4-39. *Queries with High Variation queries x-axis options*

When you hover over the dots, you receive the information based on the metric selected for the query plan as seen in Figure 4-40.

Plan Id	48
Execution Type	Completed
Plan Forced	No
Interval Start	2019-07-08 03:07:00.000 -07:00
Interval End	2019-07-08 03:08:00.000 -07:00
Execution Count	59
Total Duration (ms)	4.76
Avg Duration (ms)	0.08
Min Duration (ms)	0.03
Max Duration (ms)	0.89
Std Dev Duration (ms)	0.11
Variation Duration (ms)	1.42

Figure 4-40. *Queries with High Variation plan summary information*

You can also control the y-axis of the right-hand pane by selecting one of the options on the left-hand side as seen in Figure 4-41.

Avg
Min
Max
Std Dev
Variation

Figure 4-41. *Queries with High Variation report plan summary y-axis options*

Query Wait Statistics Report

The newest report introduced to SSMS is the Query Wait Statistics report. When you initially open the report, you get a report that shows you the total wait time by category. Query Store takes all the wait statistics and groups them into 23 categories such as CPU, memory, buffer IO, etc. Wait Statistics is a tried and true way of troubleshooting SQL Server performance and welcome addition to Query Store in SQL Server 2017. Each wait statistics category is documented in Chapter 9. An example of this report can be seen in Figure 4-42.

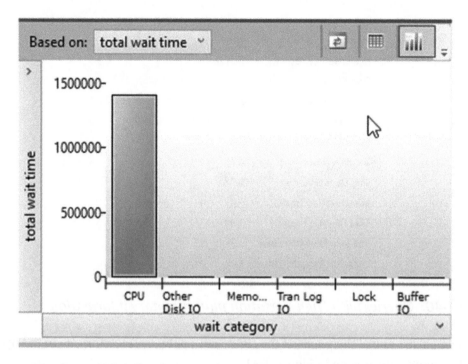

Figure 4-42. *Query Wait Statistics report categories*

The report defaults like all other reports to show wait statistics by totals, but you have the option at the top and to the left to change to the options as shown in Figure 4-43.

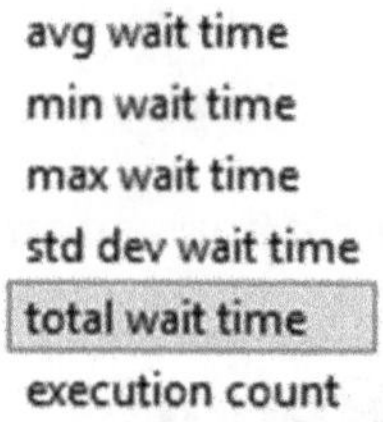

avg wait time
min wait time
max wait time
std dev wait time
total wait time
execution count

Figure 4-43. *Query Wait Statistics report categories reporting options*

At the bottom of the Chart View, you also can change the x-axis on the chart to one of the options in the drop-down as seen in Figure 4-44.

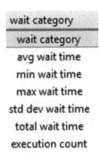

***Figure 4-44.** Query Wait Statistics report categories x-axis options*

At the top of the screen, you have three familiar buttons. The first being the Refresh button, the second being the Standard Grid button which how that looks can be seen in Figures 4-45 and 4-46, and finally, the button to change back to the Chart View.

	wait category id	wait category	avg wait time	min wait time	max wait time
1	1	CPU	715.81	0	22154
2	21	Other Disk IO	73.14	0	181
3	17	Memory	2.86	0	71
4	14	Tran Log IO	15.09	0	153
5	3	Lock	12	12	12

***Figure 4-45.** Query Wait Statistics report categories grid view*

std dev wait time	▼ total wait time	execution count
764.62	1405136	1963
50.26	4315	59
3.07	3333	1165
13.56	3153	209
1.73	12	1

***Figure 4-46.** Query Wait Statistics report categories grid view*

Once you click on one of the category bars displayed in the chart, you are shown a drilled down report of top five queries that consumed the most resources for that category as seen in Figure 4-47. This gives you the ability troubleshoot queries based on where your bottleneck appears to be based on wait statistics. If you see high CPU that would be the first on the report, then you can drill down and see the top five queries using CPU and tune those queries or see if there is a plan that can be forced that uses less resources.

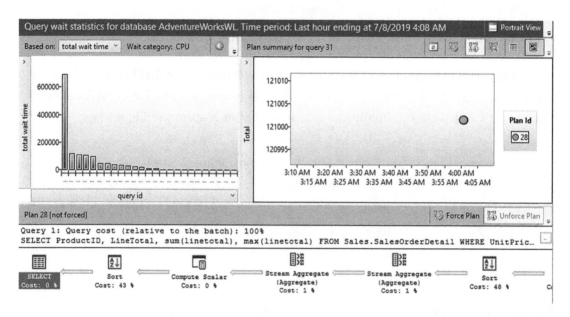

Figure 4-47. *Query Wait Statistics top five by category report*

The top bar based on drop-down has some statistics you can use to control which top five queries show up in the report as seen in Figure 4-48.

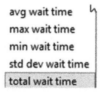

Figure 4-48. *Query Wait Statistics top five Queries Statistics*

To the right of that is a set of buttons all of them should be familiar to us by now except for the green arrow. The green arrow takes us back to the Query Wait Statistics Categories Report that we drilled down from.

Like other chart views, you can change the y-axis and x-axis attributes that are displayed; see Figures 4-49 and 4-50 for what options you have on this screen.

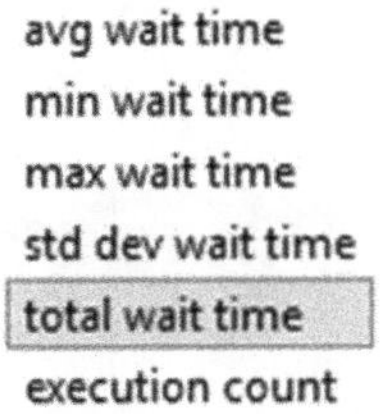

avg wait time
min wait time
max wait time
std dev wait time
total wait time
execution count

Figure 4-49. *Query Wait Statistics top five category y-axis options*

query id
query id
avg wait time
min wait time
max wait time
std dev wait time
total wait time
execution count

Figure 4-50. *Query Wait Statistics top five by Category x-axis options*

On the right-hand side pane, you have the usual dotted report representing the different plans over the period time. The buttons at the top are the same ones on the Top Resource Consuming Resource Queries Report seen in Figure 4-13. You can also change the y-axis to different statistics from the default of total to one of the values in the drop-down as seen in Figure 4-51.

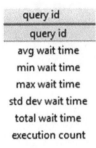

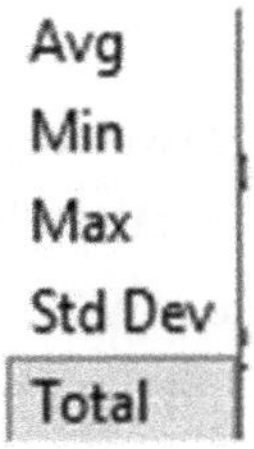

Avg
Min
Max
Std Dev
Total

Figure 4-51. *Query Wait Statistics top five by Category Plan y-axis options*

Tracked Queries Report

The Tracked Queries Report is used to show runtime statistics for a particular query you are tracking and see all the execution plans for that query. An example of a Tracked Queries Report can be seen in Figure 4-52. This is most useful when you have previously identified a query by query ID that you want to watch and see how the performance changes over time.

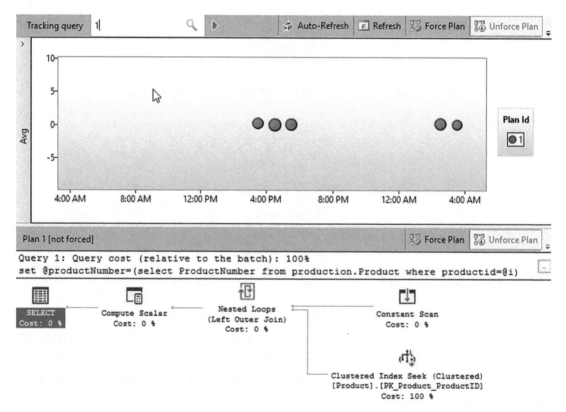

Figure 4-52. *Tracked Queries Report*

On the top left-hand corner, you have two ways to find queries that you want to track. One is to type the query ID in the white box then hit the green arrow to load the data. The data by default is for the last day. The other is to click the magnifying glass in which it will pop a window where it has loaded all the queries that have been stored in Query Store as seen in Figure 4-53.

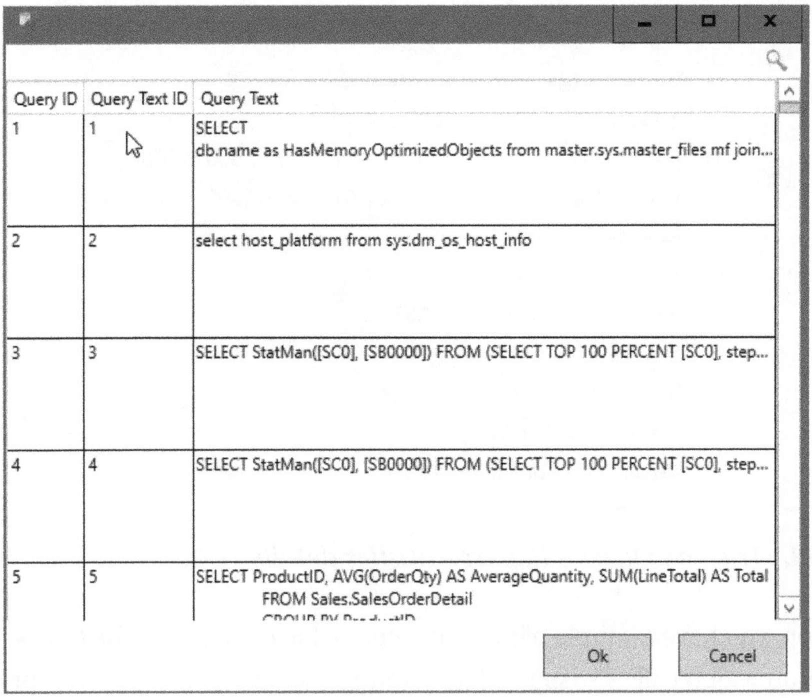

Figure 4-53. *Tracked Queries Report magnifying glass view*

From here you can select a query to track then click on OK after which you will need to hit the green arrow for it to load the data in the report. Hovering over the dots reveals the statistics for the period of time based on the metric you have configured to be shown which is the duration by default as seen in Figure 4-54.

Plan Id	4
Execution Type	Completed
Plan Forced	No
Interval Start	2019-07-07 15:00:00.000 -07:00
Interval End	2019-07-07 16:00:00.000 -07:00
Execution Count	186
Total Duration (ms)	3279.37
Avg Duration (ms)	17.63
Min Duration (ms)	0.37
Max Duration (ms)	185.34
Std Dev Duration (ms)	33.17
Variation Duration (ms)	1.88

Figure 4-54. *Tracked Queries Report statistics details*

At the top, you have a couple of new buttons we have not seen. The first is the Auto Refresh button which will as suspected auto refreshes the report every 5 seconds. The Auto Refresh setting is configurable under the Configure button. There is only one other configurable setting in that screen we have not seen, and that is which query to track which can change from there.

Conclusion

In this chapter we looked at the Regressed Queries, Overall Resource Consumption, Top Resource Consumption Queries, Queries with Forced Plans, Queries with High Variation, Query Wait Statistics, and Tracked Queries reports and how they interacted with each other. We explored all the options you had available to change what data is reported on the screen and how to configure each report to meet your needs. These reports are vital to quickly being able to troubleshoot issues with Query Store on your SQL Server instance.

CHAPTER 5

Query Store Catalog Views

Query Store introduces eight new catalog views to SQL Server where it stores all the information you need to query data to troubleshoot SQL Server with Query Store and check the configuration of Query Store. You need VIEW DATABASE STATE permission to query the catalog views. In this chapter you will find descriptions of all the catalog views and their columns then examples of the queries behind the standard Query Store reports we discussed in Chapter 4.

sys.database_query_store_options

The catalog view that holds the options that tell you the settings for the setup of Query Store is sys.database_query_store_options. This catalog view returns all the options available that are set for the configuration of Query Store. This catalog view has no relationships with any of the other catalog views. Sometimes you need to check the configuration of Query Store across all your databases where Query Store is turned on; you can use the query in Listing 5-1 to return a result set for each database that has Query Store enabled with all the settings.

© Tracy Boggiano and Grant Fritchey 2019

T. Boggiano and G. Fritchey, *Query Store for SQL Server 2019*, https://doi.org/10.1007/978-1-4842-5004-4_5

Listing 5-1. Check Query Store options across all databases on a SQL Server instance

```
DECLARE @SQL NVARCHAR(MAX) = '';

SELECT @SQL += REPLACE(REPLACE('
    USE [{{DBName}}];
    SELECT "{{DBName}}",
        *
    FROM sys.database_query_store_options; '
    ,'{{DBName}}', [name])
    ,'"','''')
FROM sys.databases
WHERE is_query_store_on = 1;

EXEC (@SQL);
```

Table 5-1 displays all the column names, data types, and descriptions for the columns in the sys.database_query_store_options catalog view. Important columns to keep an eye on are the actual_state_desc; you want to make sure it stays in READ_WRITE if the desired_state is READ_WRITE and did not switch to READ_ONLY due to running out of space or ERROR. To understand these options for these columns better, please refer to Chapter 3.

Table 5-1. Column listing and descriptions for sys.database_query_store options

Column name	Data type	Description
desired_state	smallint	Shows the desired state of Query Store. These are the only values that can be set by the user. Valid values are as follows: 0 = OFF 1 = READ_ONLY 2 = READ_WRITE
desired_state_desc	nvarchar(60)	Gives you a description of the desired state of Query Store. Valid values are as follows: OFF READ_ONLY READ_WRITE
actual_state	smallint	Shows the actual state of Query Store. Note the additional value of ERROR that was not available in the desired state. Valid values are as follows: 0 = OFF 1 = READ_ONLY 2 = READ_WRITE 3 = ERROR
actual_state_desc	nvarchar(60)	Gives you a description of the actual state of Query Store. Valid values are as follows: OFF READ_ONLY READ_WRITE ERROR

(continued)

Table 5-1. (*continued*)

Column name	Data type	Description
readonly_reason	int	When the database is in READ_ONLY mode, but the desired state is READ_WRITE, a bitmap is stored in the column to indicate the reason why. Valid values are as follows:
		1 – the database has been placed in the read-only mode
		2 – the database has been placed in the single-user mode
		4 – the database has been placed in the emergency mode
		8 – the database is a secondary replica. This applies for Availability Groups and Azure SQL Database geo-replicated databases because essentially all secondary replicas are read-only copies of the databases
		65536 – the max size limit specified in MAX_STORAGE_SIZE_MB has been reached
		46410 – in Azure SQL Database, there is a limit as to how many queries can be stored in internal memory, so this indicates you have reached that limit. You may upgrade to a higher service tier to get a higher limit or remove queries you no longer need from Query Store used in stored procedure sys.sp_query_store_remove_query
		262144 – In Azure SQL Database there is the potential to reach a limit to the amount of data that will be held in memory before it persists to disk. During that time Query Store will be temporarily put in READ_ONLY mode
		524288 – in Azure SQL Database, the database has run out of space
		To fix any of these conditions, please refer to Chapter 3 on Configuring Query Store
current_storage_size_mb	bigint	Tells you the current size of Query Store is used in MBs

Column	Type	Description
flush_interval_seconds	bigint	Tells you how often Query Store is persisting data to disk. The default is 900 seconds (15 minutes)
interval_length_minutes	bigint	Tells Query Store what intervals to roll up the statistics into. The following are valid values: 1, 5, 10, 15, 30, 60, and 1440 minutes. The default value is 60 minutes
max_storage_size_mb	bigint	Tells Query Store the maximum amount of disk space that it can use
stale_query_threshold_days	bigint	The number of days a query stays in Query Store. The default value is 30 days. If you set the value to 0, it will disable the retention policy. For Azure SQL Database Basic Edition, the default value is 7 days
max_plans_per_query	bigint	The maximum number of plans Query Store will keep for each query. Once the maximum number is reached, Query Store no longer captures plans for that query. If you set the value to 0, it will have no limitation Applies to SQL Server 2017 and up
query_capture_mode	smallint	The capture mode for Query Store. Valid values are as follows: 1 = ALL – captures all queries. (Default for SQL Server 2016 and up) 2 = AUTO – captures queries based on the usage patterns. (Default for Azure SQL Database) 3 = NONE – tells Query Store to stop capturing new queries. Query Store however continues to collect statistics for queries already in Query Store 4 = CUSTOM – tells Query Store to use custom configurations options to determine what queries to store (applies to SQL Server 2019 only)

Table 5-1. (*continued*)

Column name	Data type	Description
query_capture_mode_desc	nvarchar(60)	Description of the capture mode of Query Store. Valid values are as follows: ALL AUTO CUSTOM (applies to SQL Server 2019 only) NONE
capture_policy_execution_count	int	Number of times a query executes while query capture mode is CUSTOM before it is captured (applies to SQL Server 2019 only)
capture_policy_total_compile_cpu_time_ms	bigint	Total CPU compile time in ms before is captured while query capture mode is CUSTOM (applies to SQL Server 2019 only)
capture_policy_total_execution_cpu_time_ms	bigint	Total CPU execution time in ms before is captured while query capture mode is CUSTOM (applies to SQL Server 2019 only)
capture_policy_state_threshold_hours	int	The amount of time queries will collect data while query capture mode is CUSTOM to determine if the query stats should be captured (applies to SQL Server 2019 only)
size_based_cleanup_mode	smallint	Tells Query Store rather or not to clean up Query Store when it gets close to the maximum size. Valid values are as follows: 0 = OFF – do not clean up automatically 1 = AUTO – clean up automatically when 90% of the maximum size is reached. This is the default value. The least expensive and oldest queries are removed first until it reaches about 80% free space

size_based_cleanup_mode_desc	nvarchar(60)	Description of size-based cleanup. Valid values are as follows: OFF AUTO
wait_stats_capture_mode	smallint	Tells Query Store to capture wait statistics or not. Valid values are as follows: 0 = OFF 1 = ON Applies to SQL Server 2017 and up
wait_stats_capture_mode_desc	nvarchar(60)	Description of rather wait statistics are captured or not. Valid values are as follows: OFF ON (default) Applies to SQL Server 2017 and up
actual_state_additional_info	nvarchar(8000)	Additional information on how Query Store ended up in the current state. Usually populated when in the state is not in the expected state

sys.query_context_settings

The sys.query_context_settings catalog view holds the context settings that the queries in Query Store were running with such ANSI_NULLS or QUOTED_IDENTIFIER. If different context settings are used with the same query, you will end up with different plans in Query Store. A bit mask is stored in the set_options field to tell us which options were used when a query was run. There are two ways to view the set options for a query. The first is to use the Dynamic Management Function sys.dm_exec_plan_atttibutes and pass in the plan_handle. This method only works if the plan is still in the plan cache. In Listing 5-2 you can retrieve a plan_handle or context_settings_id for a particular query by narrowing down your selection by feeling part of the query in the WHERE clause in the <value> placeholder.

Listing 5-2. Query to retrieve a plan handle from cache

```
SELECT
      q.query_id,
      qt.query_sql_text,
      qs.plan_handle,
      q.context_settings_id
FROM sys.query_store_query q
      INNER JOIN sys.dm_exec_query_stats qs
            ON q.last_compile_batch_sql_handle =
                  qs.sql_handle
      INNER JOIN sys.query_store_query_text qt
            ON q.query_text_id = qt.query_text_id
      INNER JOIN sys.query_context_settings cs
            ON cs.context_settings_id = q.context_settings_id
WHERE qt.query_sql_text LIKE '%<value>%'
ORDER BY q.query_id
```

Next, you copy the plan handle for the query you want to see the set options for and put in Listing 5-3 replacing <plan_handle> in the listing.

Listing 5-3. Retrieve set options for a plan handle

```
SELECT *
FROM sys.dm_exec_plan_attributes(<plan_handle>)
WHERE attribute = 'set_options'
```

Second, you can create a function then you can query a record from the catalog view and use the context_settings_id returned in Listing 5-2 as the @SetOptions value to view the set options that were used as seen in Listing 5-4.

Listing 5-4. Function to retrieve SET options for queries executed

```
CREATE FUNCTION fn_QueryStoreSetOptions (@SetOptions as int)
RETURNS VARCHAR(MAX)
AS
BEGIN
    DECLARE @Result VARCHAR(MAX)=",
        @SetOptionFound INT
    DECLARE @SetOptionsList TABLE
    (
        [Value] INT,
        [Option] VARCHAR(60)
    )

    INSERT INTO @SetOptionsList
    VALUES
    (1,'ANSI_PADDING'),
    (2,'Parallel Plan'),
    (4, 'FORCEPLAN'),
    (8, 'CONCAT_NULL_YIELDS_NULL'),
    (16, 'ANSI_WARNINGS'),
    (32, 'ANSI_NULLS'),
    (64, 'QUOTED_IDENTIFIER'),
    (128, 'ANSI_NULL_DFLT_ON'),
    (256, 'ANSI_NULL_DFLT_OFF'),
    (512, 'NoBrowseTable'),
    (1024, 'TriggerOneRow'),
    (2048, 'ResyncQuery'),
```

```
    (4096,'ARITH_ABORT'),
    (8192,'NUMERIC_ROUNDABORT'),
    (16384,'DATEFIRST'),
    (32768,'DATEFORMAT'),
    (65536,'LanguageID'),
    (131072,'UPON'),
    (262144,'ROWCOUNT')

SELECT TOP 1 @SetOptionFound = ISNULL([Value], -1),
        @Result = ISNULL([Option] , '') + '; '
FROM @SetOptionsList
WHERE [Value] <= @SetOptions
ORDER BY [Value] DESC

RETURN @Result +
    CASE WHEN @SetOptionFound > -1 THEN
            dbo.fn_QueryStoreSetOptions(@SetOptions -
                @SetOptionFound)
            ELSE ''
        END
END
GO
```

Next, we need to query the sys.query_context_settings catalog view and CAST the set_options column to an INT value to parse the SET options as seen in Listing 5-5. You can see an example of the output of the results in Figure 5-1.

Listing 5-5. Query to return SET options for a query executed

```
SELECT dbo.fn_QueryStoreSetOptions(CAST(set_options as int))
FROM sys.query_context_settings
```

set_options
ARITH_ABORT; ANSI_NULL_DFLT_ON; QUOTED_IDENTIFIER; ANSI_NULLS; ANSI_WARNINGS; CONCAT_NULL_YIELDS_NULL; Parallel Plan; ANSI_PADDING;

Figure 5-1. *Set options query results*

Table 5-2 displays all the column names, data types, and descriptions for the columns in the sys.query_context_settings catalog view.

Table 5-2. *Column listing and descriptions for sys.query_context_settings*

Column name	Data type	Description
context_settings_id	bigint	Primary key. This value is in the Showplan XML queries for reference
set_options	varbinary(8)	Bit mask reflecting SET options. Values for bit mask values are calculated using the following: 1 – ANSI_PADDING 2 – Parallel Plan 4 – FORCEPLAN 8 – CONCAT_NULL_YIELDS_NULL 16 – ANSI_WARNINGS 32 – ANSI_NULLS 64 – QUOTED_IDENTIFIER 128 – ANSI_NULL_DFLT_ON 256 – ANSI_NULL_DFLT_OFF 512 – NoBrowseTable 1024 – TriggerOneRow 2048 – ResyncQuery 4096 – ARITH_ABORT 8192 – NUMERIC_ROUNDABORT 16384 – DATEFIRST 32768 – DATEFORMAT 65536 – LanguageID 131072 – UPON 262144 – ROWCOUNT
language_id	smallint	The ID of the language. Look for more information online by looking at the sys.languages table
date_format	smallint	The date format. See the SET DATEFORMAT command for more information
date_first	smallint	The date first value. See the SET DATEFIRST command for more information

(continued)

Table 5-2. (*continued*)

Column name	Data type	Description
status	varbinary(2)	Bit mask field indicating the type of query or context in which it was executed. Value can be any combination of flags in hexadecimal: 0x0 – regular query (no specific flags) 0x1 – query that was executed through on or the cursor APIs' stored procedures 0x2 – query for notification 0x4 – internal query 0x8 – auto parameterized query without universal parameterization 0x10 – cursor fetch refresh query 0x20 – a query that is being used in cursor update requests 0x40 – initial result set is returned when a cursor is opened (Cursor Auto Fetch) 0x80 – encrypted query 0x100 – query in context of row-level security predicate
required_cursor_options	int	Options specified for cursor
acceptable_cursor_options	int	Options SQL Server may implicitly convert a cursor to support the execution of the statement
merge_action_type	smallint	A MERGE statement trigger execution plan is used. Valid values are as follows: 0 – no trigger or executes as a DELETE action. 1 – INSERT plan. 2 – UPDATE plan. 3 – DELETE plan with the addition of an INSERT or UPDATE action
default_schema_id	int	ID of the default schema, which is used to resolve names that are not fully qualified names
is_replication_specific	bit	Used for replication
is_contained	varbinary(1)	1 indicates a contained database

sys.query_store_plan

The sys.query_store_plan catalog view stores the query plan associated with each query in Query Store. The most important column in this catalog view is the query_plan column as it shows you the execution plan that was stored for the query. You can copy and paste this into an editor of your choice and save with a .sqlplan extension and open with SSMS to view the graphical execution plan. Two other interesting columns are the engine_version and compatibility_level columns. The engine_version column lets us know what the exact version of SQL Server that was running when the query plan was captured. This is useful for troubleshooting plan regression due to upgrades. The compatibility_level column tells which compatibility level the query was ran under. This is useful when upgrading as well but especially when going from a compatibility level below SQL Server 2014 to SQL Server 2014 and up due to the cardinality estimator (CE) changes made in SQL Server 2014. Table 5-3 displays all the column names, data types, and descriptions for the columns in the sys.query_store_plan catalog view.

Table 5-3. *Column listing and descriptions for sys.query_store_plan*

Column Name	Data Type	Description
plan_id	bigint	Primary key
query_id	bigint	Foreign key to sys.query_store_query. Refer to Table 5-4
plan_group_id	bigint	ID of plan group. Multiple plans are often created for cursor queries. The same group will contain the populate and fetch plans
engine_version	nvarchar(32)	Version of SQL Server for the compiled plan "major.minor.build.revision" format
compatibility_level	smallint	Compatibility level of the database when the query was ran
query_plan_hash	varbinary(8)	MD5 hash of the query plan
query_plan	nvarchar(max)	Showplan XML for the query plan
is_online_index_plan	bit	Indicates rather the plan was used during an online index rebuild

(continued)

113

Table 5-3. (*continued*)

Column Name	Data Type	Description
is_trivial_plan	bit	The plan is a trivial plan
is_parallel_plan	bit	The plan is parallel plan
is_forced_plan	bit	The plan is a forced plan marked by using stored procedure sys.sp_query_store_forced_plan. Plan forcing does not guarantee this exact plan will be used. The query compiles and compares the new compiled plan to the one that was forced. If it fails to match, the column force_failure_count increments and the column last_force_failure_reason will record the reason
is_natively_compiled	bit	The plan includes natively compiled memory-optimized procedure. Valid values are as follows: 0 – false 1 – true
force_failure_count	bigint	The number of times that forcing this plan has failed
last_force_failure_reason	int	Last reason why plan forcing failed. Valid values are as follows: 0 – no failure 8637 – ONLINE_INDEX_BUILD 8683 – INVALID_STARJOIN 8684 – TIME_OUT 8689 – NO_DB 8690 – HINT_CONFLICT 8691 – SETOPT_CONFLICT 8694 – DQ_NO_FORCING_SUPPORTED 8698 – NO_PLAN 8712 – NO_INDEX 8713 – VIEW_COMPILE_FAILED <other value> – GENERAL_FAILURE

(*continued*)

Table 5-3. (*continued*)

Column Name	Data Type	Description
last_force_failure_ reason_desc	nvarchar(128)	Description of last force plan failure. Valid values are as follows: ONLINE_INDEX_BUILD – online rebuild was occurring on the a table in the query while the query was trying to modify data
		INVALID_STARJOIN – contains invalid StarJoin TIME_OUT – forced plan could not be found by the optimizer in the number of allowed operations HINT_CONFLICT – query hint conflicts prevented the query from being compiled DQ_NO_FORCING_SUPPORTED – plan conflicts with the use of a distributed query or full-text operations NO_PLAN – forced plan could not be verified so the query processor did not produce a query plan NO_INDEX – index specified in the plan no longer exists VIEW_COMPILE_FAILED – problem exists in an indexed view referenced in the plan GENERAL_FAILURE – general forcing error
count_compiles	bigint	The number of compiles
initial_compile_start_ time	datetimeoffset	Initial compile start time
last_compile_start_ time	datetimeoffset	Last compile start time
last_execution_time	datetimeoffset	Last execution time
avg_compile_duration	float	Average compile duration

(*continued*)

Table 5-3. (*continued*)

Column Name	Data Type	Description
last_compiled_duration	bigint	Last compile duration
plan_forcing_type	int	Plan forcing type 0 – NONE 1 – MANUAL 2 – AUTO
plan_forcing_type_desc	nvarchar(60)	Text description of plan_forcing_type NONE – no plan forcing MANUAL – plan forced by user AUTO – plan forced by automatic tuning

Note   When querying using the `datetimeoffset` datatypes, you need to specify the time zone the data was generated in to see the data at the times it was generated because all data is stored in UTC time in this datatype.

sys.query_store_query

All metrics per query executed are stored inside this catalog view. The data in the catalog view is stored at the SQL statement level. Batches are split up into statements in the catalog view allowing for better troubleshooting. Most of the columns in the catalog view are metrics for compiling and binding the plan for the statements. Of note in this catalog view is the `object_id` column. This column allows you to tie the statements back to their stored procedure, function, or trigger. Table 5-4 shows all the column names, data types, and descriptions for the columns in the `sys.query_store_query` catalog view.

Table 5-4. *Column listing and descriptions for sys.query_store_query*

Column name	Data type	Description
query_id	bigint	Primary key
query_text_id	bigint	Foreign key to sys.query_store_query_text. Refer to Table 5-5
context_settings_id	bigint	Foreign key to sys.query_context_settings. Refer to Table 5-2
object_id	bigint	ID of the database object. Value will be 0 for ad-hoc queries
batch_sql_handle	varbinary(64)	ID of the statement batch the query is part of. Populated only if the query references temporary tables or table variables
query_hash	binary(8)	MD5 hash of the query including optimizer hints
is_internal_query	bit	The query was generated internally
query_paramterization_type	tinyint	Kind of parameterization: 0 – none 1 – user 2 – simple 3 – forced
query_paramterization_type_desc	nvarchar(60)	Text description of type of parameterization
initial_compile_start_time	datetimeoffset	Initial compile start time
last_compile_start_time	datetimeoffset	Last compile start time
last_execution_time	datetimeoffset	Last execution time
last_compile_batch_sql_handle	varbinary(64)	Last SQL batch handle for this query. It can be used with sys.dm_exec_sql_text to get the full text of the batch

(*continued*)

Table 5-4. (*continued*)

Column name	Data type	Description
last_compile_batch_offset_start	bigint	Last start compile batch line number
last_compile_batch_offset_end	bigint	Last end compile batch line number
count_compiles	bigint	The number of compiles
avg_compile_duration	float	Average compile time in microseconds
last_compile_duration	bigint	Last compile time in microseconds
avg_bind_duration	float	Average bind time in microseconds
last_bind_duration	bigint	Last bind time in microseconds
avg_bind_cpu_time	float	Average bind CPU time in microseconds
last_bind_cpu_time	bigint	Last bind CPU time in microseconds
avg_optimize_duration	float	Average optimize time in microseconds
last_optimize_duration	bigint	Last optimize time in microseconds
avg_optimize_cpu_time	float	Average optimize CPU time in microseconds
last_optimize_cpu_time	bigint	Last optimize CPU time in microseconds
avg_compile_memory_kb	float	Average compile memory in kilobytes
last_compile_memory_kb	bigint	Last compile memory in kilobytes
max_compile_memory_kb	bigint	Max compile memory in kilobytes
is_clouddb_internal_query	bit	Always 0 on on-premises instances

sys.query_store_query_text

The sys.query_store_query_text catalog view contains the query text of the SQL
Statement to be joined to sys.query_store_query catalog view to get statement level
data, not batch level data. Using the object_id from sys.query_store_query, we are in
Listing 5-6 querying for all the statements for an object by subbing in an object name in
the placeholder <object_name>.

Listing 5-6. Retrieve statements for an object

```
SELECT *
FROM sys.query_store_query_text qt
     INNER JOIN sys.query_store_query q
             ON q.query_text_id = qt.query_text_id
     INNER JOIN sys.objects o on o.object_id = q.object_id
WHERE o.name = '<object_name>'
```

Table 5-5 shows all the column names, data types, and descriptions for the columns in the sys.query_store_query_text catalog view.

Table 5-5. *Column listing and descriptions for sys.query_store_query_text*

Column name	Data type	Description
query_text_id	bigint	Primary key
query_sql_text	nvarchar(max)	SQL text of the query as provided by user
statement_sql_handle	varbinary(64)	SQL handle of the query
is_part_of_encrypted_module	bit	Indicates if the query is part of an encrypted module
has_restricted_text	bit	Indicates if the query text contains passwords or other unmentionable words

sys.query_store_wait_stats

The sys.query_store_wait_stats catalog view was introduced to Query Store in SQL Server 2017 and gave us major insights into what each query was waiting on when executing. In Listing 5-7 you can see a summary of the wait statistics collected across categories for the statements in an object by subbing in value for <object_name>.

Listing 5-7. Wait stats for statements in an object

```
SELECT *
FROM sys.query_store_query_text qt
     INNER JOIN sys.query_store_query q
             ON q.query_text_id = qt.query_text_id
```

```
        INNER JOIN sys.objects o on o.object_id = q.object_id
        INNER JOIN sys.query_store_plan p
            ON p.query_id = q.query_id
        INNER JOIN sys.query_store_wait_stats ws
            ON ws.plan_id = p.plan_id
WHERE o.name = '<object_name>'
```

Below in Table 5-6 are all the column names, data types, and descriptions for the columns in the sys.query_store_wait_stats catalog view.

Table 5-6. *Column listing and descriptions for sys.query_store_wait_stats*

Column name	Data type	Description
wait_stats_id	bigint	Identifier of the row representing wait statistics for the plan_id, runtime_stats_interval_id, execution_type, and wait_category. It is unique only for the past runtime statistics intervals. For currently active intervals, there may be multiple rows representing one row of statistics flushed to disk and possible multiple rows for data still held in memory
plan_id	bigint	Foreign key to sys.query_store_plan. Refer to Table 5-3
runtime_stats_interval_id	bigint	Foreign key to sys.query_store_runtime_stats_interval. Refer to Table 5-8
wait_category	tinyint	Represents what category wait time is aggregated into. Refer to Table 5-7 for wait statistics type mappings and valid values
wait_category_desc	nvarchar(128)	Description of the wait statistics category. Refer to Table 5-7 for wait statistics type mappings and valid values

(continued)

Table 5-6. (*continued*)

Column name	Data type	Description
execution_type	tinyint	Determines the type of query execution. Valid values are as follows: 0 – regular execution: successful 3 – client aborted the execution 4 – exception aborted execution
execution_type_desc	nvarchar(128)	Textual description of the execution type field. Valid values are as follows: 0 – regular 3 – aborted 4 – exception
total_query_wait_time_ms	bigint	Total CPU wait time in the aggregation interval in milliseconds
avg_query_wait_time_ms	float	Average CPU wait duration per execution in the aggregation interval in milliseconds
last_query_wait_time_ms	bigint	Last CPU wait duration in the aggregation interval in milliseconds
min_query_wait_time_ms	bigint	Minimum CPU wait time in the aggregation interval in milliseconds
max_query_wait_time_ms	bigint	Maximum CPU wait time in the aggregation interval in milliseconds
stdev_query_wait_time_ms	float	Standard deviation CPU wait time in the aggregation interval in milliseconds

Wait statistics are divided into 23 categories a list of which can be found in Table 5-7 with a list of which wait statistics belong in each category.

Table 5-7. *Wait statistics categories mapping table*

Wait statistics ID	Wait statistics category description	Wait statistics types included in the category
0	Unknown	Unknown
1	CPU	SOS_SCHEDULER_YIELD
2	Worker thread	THREADPOOL
3	Lock	LCK_M_%
4	Latch	LATCH_%
5	Buffer latch	PAGELATCH_%
6	Buffer IO	PAGEIOLATCH_%
7	Compilation*	RESOURCE_SEMAPHORE_QUERY_COMPILE
8	SQL CLR	CLR%, SQLCLR%
9	Mirroring	DBMIRROR%
10	Transaction	XACT%, DTC%, TRAN_MARKLATCH_%, MSQL_XACT_%, TRANSACTION_MUTEX
11	Idle	SLEEP_%, LAZYWRITER_SLEEP, SQLTRACE_BUFFER_FLUSH, SQLTRACE_INCREMENTAL_FLUSH_SLEEP, SQLTRACE_WAIT_ENTRIES, FT_IFTS_SCHEDULER_IDLE_WAIT, XE_DISPATCHER_WAIT, REQUEST_FOR_DEADLOCK_SEARCH, LOGMGR_QUEUE, ONDEMAND_TASK_QUEUE, CHECKPOINT_QUEUE, XE_TIMER_EVENT
12	Preemptive	PREEMPTIVE_%
13	Service broker	BROKER_% (but not BROKER_RECEIVE_WAITFOR)
14	Tran Log IO	LOGMGR, LOGBUFFER, LOGMGR_RESERVE_APPEND, LOGMGR_FLUSH, LOGMGR_PMM_LOG, CHKPT, WRITELOGF
15	Network IO	ASYNC_NETWORK_IO, NET_WAITFOR_PACKET, PROXY_NETWORK_IO, EXTERNAL_SCRIPT_NETWORK_IOF
16	Parallelism	CXPACKET, EXCHANGE

(continued)

Table 5-7. (*continued*)

Wait statistics ID	Wait statistics category description	Wait statistics types included in the category
17	Memory	RESOURCE_SEMAPHORE, CMEMTHREAD, CMEMPARTITIONED, EE_PMOLOCK, MEMORY_ALLOCATION_EXT, RESERVED_MEMORY_ALLOCATION_EXT, MEMORY_GRANT_UPDATE
18	User wait	WAITFOR, WAIT_FOR_RESULTS, BROKER_RECEIVE_WAITFOR
19	Tracing	TRACEWRITE, SQLTRACE_LOCK, SQLTRACE_FILE_BUFFER, SQLTRACE_FILE_WRITE_IO_COMPLETION, SQLTRACE_FILE_READ_IO_COMPLETION, SQLTRACE_PENDING_BUFFER_WRITERS, SQLTRACE_SHUTDOWN, QUERY_TRACEOUT, TRACE_EVTNOTIFF
20	Full text search	FT_RESTART_CRAWL, FULLTEXT GATHERER, MSSEARCH, FT_METADATA_MUTEX, FT_IFTSHC_MUTEX, FT_IFTSISM_MUTEX, FT_IFTS_RWLOCK, FT_COMPROWSET_RWLOCK, FT_MASTER_MERGE, FT_PROPERTYLIST_CACHE, FT_MASTER_MERGE_COORDINATOR, PWAIT_RESOURCE_SEMAPHORE_FT_PARALLEL_QUERY_SYNC
21	Other disk IO	ASYNC_IO_COMPLETION, IO_COMPLETION, BACKUPIO, WRITE_COMPLETION, IO_QUEUE_LIMIT, IO_RETRY
22	Replication	SE_REPL_%, REPL_%, HADR_% **(but not HADR_THROTTLE_LOG_RATE_GOVERNOR),** PWAIT_HADR_%, REPLICA_WRITES, FCB_REPLICA_WRITE, FCB_REPLICA_READ, PWAIT_HADRSIM
23	Log rate governor	LOG_RATE_GOVERNOR, POOL_LOG_RATE_GOVERNOR, HADR_THROTTLE_LOG_RATE_GOVERNOR, INSTANCE_LOG_RATE_GOVERNOR

*Currently not supported.

sys.query_store_runtime_stats

The sys.query_store_runtime_stats catalog view contains the runtime stats for all
the plans that Query Store has store aggregated by the runtime_stats_interval_id.
Statistics it collects include average, last, minimum, maximum, and standard deviation
for the duration, CPU, logical IO, physical IO, CLR, DOP (degree of parallelism),
query max used memory, row count, and for Azure SQL Database log bytes used.
Besides the wait statistics catalog view, this catalog view is where you harvest the most
data. Listing 5-8 will return the top 10 queries by average duration that have a last_
execution_time in the last hour.

Listing 5-8. Top 10 queries by CPU in the last hour

```
SELECT TOP 10 sum(rs.count_executions * rs.avg_duration) avg_duration,
     qt.query_sql_text,
     q.query_id,
     qt.query_text_id,
     p.plan_id,
     rs.last_execution_time
FROM sys.query_store_query_text AS qt
INNER JOIN sys.query_store_query AS q
   ON qt.query_text_id = q.query_text_id
INNER JOIN sys.query_store_plan AS p
   ON q.query_id = p.query_id
INNER JOIN sys.query_store_runtime_stats AS rs
   ON p.plan_id = rs.plan_id
WHERE rs.last_execution_time > DATEADD(hour, -1, GETUTCDATE())
GROUP BY qt.query_sql_text,
     q.query_id,
     qt.query_text_id,
     p.plan_id,
     rs.last_execution_time
ORDER BY avg_duration DESC;
```

Table 5-8 shows all the column names, data types, and descriptions for the columns
in the sys.query_store_runtime_stats catalog view.

Table 5-8. *Column listing and descriptions for sys.query_store_runtime_stats*

Column name	Data type	Description
runtime_stats_id	Bigint	Identifier of the row representing runtime execution statistics for the `plan_id`, `execution_type`, and `runtime_stats_interval_id`. It is unique only for the past runtime statistics intervals. For currently active intervals, there may be multiple rows representing one row of statistics flushed to disk and possible multiple rows for data still held in memory
plan_id	Bigint	Foreign key to `sys.query_store_plan` refers to Table 5-3
runtime_stats_interval_id	Bigint	Foreign key to `sys.query_store_runtime_stats_interval` refers to Table 5-9
execution_type	tinyint	Determines the type of query execution. Valid values are as follows: 0 – regular execution: successful 3 – client aborted the execution 4 – exception aborted execution
execution_type_desc	nvarchar(128)	Textual description of the execution type field. Valid values are as follows: 0 – regular 3 – aborted 4 – exception
first_execution_time	datetimeoffset	First execution time for the query plan within the aggregation interval
last_execution_time	datetimeoffset	Last execution time for the query plan within the aggregation interval
count_executions	bigint	Total count of executions for the query plan within the aggregation interval

(continued)

Table 5-8. (*continued*)

Column name	Data type	Description
avg_duration	float	The average duration for the query plan within the aggregation interval in microseconds
last_duration	bigint	The last duration for the query plan within the aggregation interval in microseconds
min_duration	bigint	The minimum duration for the query plan within the aggregation interval in microseconds
max_duration	bigint	The maximum duration for the query plan within the aggregation interval in microseconds
stdev_duration	float	The standard deviation duration for the query plan within the aggregation interval in microseconds
avg_cpu_time	float	The average CPU time for the query plan within the aggregation interval in microseconds
last_cpu_time	bigint	The last CPU time for the query plan within the aggregation interval in microseconds
min_cpu_time	bigint	The minimum CPU time for the query plan within the aggregation interval in microseconds
max_cpu_time	bigint	The maximum CPU time for the query plan within the aggregation interval in microseconds
stdev_cpu_time	float	The standard deviation CPU time for the query plan within the aggregation interval in microseconds
avg_logical_io_reads	float	The average number of logical IO reads for the query plan within the aggregation interval in 8KB pages
last_logical_io_reads	bigint	The last number of logical IO reads for the query plan within the aggregation interval in 8KB pages

(*continued*)

Table 5-8. (*continued*)

Column name	Data type	Description
min_logical_io_reads	bigint	The minimum number of logical IO reads for the query plan within the aggregation interval in 8KB pages
max_logical_io_reads	bigint	The maximum number of logical IO reads for the query plan within the aggregation interval in 8KB pages
stdev_logical_io_reads	float	The standard deviation number of logical IO reads for the query plan within the aggregation interval in 8KB pages
avg_logical_io_writes	float	The average number of logical IO writes for the query plan within the aggregation interval
last_logical_io_writes	bigint	The last number of logical IO writes for the query plan within the aggregation interval
min_logical_io_writes	bigint	The minimum number of logical IO writes for the query plan within the aggregation interval
max_logical_io_writes	bigint	The maximum number of logical IO writes for the query plan within the aggregation interval
stdev_logical_io_writes	float	The standard deviation number of logical IO writes for the query plan within the aggregation interval
avg_physical_io_reads	float	The average number of physical IO reads for the query plan within the aggregation interval in 8KB pages
last_physical_io_reads	bigint	The last number of physical IO reads for the query plan within the aggregation interval in 8KB pages
min_physical_io_reads	bigint	The minimum number of physical IO reads for the query plan within the aggregation interval in 8KB pages

(*continued*)

Table 5-8. (*continued*)

Column name	Data type	Description
max_physical_io_reads	bigint	The maximum number of physical IO reads for the query plan within the aggregation interval in 8KB pages
stdev_physical_io_reads	float	The standard deviation number of physical IO reads for the query plan within the aggregation interval in 8KB pages
avg_clr_time	float	The average CLR time for the query plan within the aggregation interval in microseconds
last_clr_time	bigint	The last CLR time for the query plan within the aggregation interval in microseconds
min_clr_time	bigint	The minimum CLR time for the query plan within the aggregation interval in microseconds
max_clr_time	bigint	The maximum CLR time for the query plan within the aggregation interval in microseconds
stdev_clr_time	float	The standard deviation CLR time for the query plan within the aggregation interval in microseconds
avg_dop_time	float	The average DOP (degree of parallelism) for the query plan within the aggregation interval in microseconds
last_dop_time	bigint	The last DOP for the query plan within the aggregation interval in microseconds
min_dop_time	bigint	The minimum DOP for the query plan within the aggregation interval in microseconds
max_dop_time	bigint	The maximum DOP for the query plan within the aggregation interval in microseconds
stdev_dop_time	float	The standard deviation DOP for the query plan within the aggregation interval in microseconds

(*continued*)

Table 5-8. (*continued*)

Column name	Data type	Description
avg_query_max_used_memory	float	The average memory grant for the query plan within the aggregation interval in 8 KB pages. Always 0 for queries using natively compiled memory optimized procedures
last_query_max_used_memory	bigint	The last memory grant for the query plan within the aggregation interval in 8 KB pages. Always 0 for queries using natively compiled memory optimized procedures
min_query_max_used_ memory	bigint	The minimum memory grant for the query plan within the aggregation interval in 8 KB pages. Always 0 for queries using natively compiled memory optimized procedures
max_query_max_used_ memory	bigint	The maximum memory grant for the query plan within the aggregation interval in 8 KB pages. Always 0 for queries using natively compiled memory optimized procedures
stdev_query_max_used_ memory	float	The standard deviation memory grant for the query plan within the aggregation interval in 8 KB pages. Always 0 for queries using natively compiled memory optimized procedures
avg_rowcount	float	The average number of returned rows for the query plan within the aggregation interval
last_rowcount	bigint	The last number of returned rows for the query plan within the aggregation interval
min_rowcount	bigint	The minimum number of returned rows for the query plan within the aggregation interval
max_rowcount	bigint	The maximum number of returned rows for the query plan within the aggregation interval

(*continued*)

Table 5-8. (*continued*)

Column name	Data type	Description
stdev_rowcount	float	The standard deviation number of returned rows for the query plan within the aggregation interval
avg_log_bytes_used	float	The average number of bytes in the database log used by the query plan within the aggregation interval. Applies **only to Azure SQL Database**
last_log_bytes_used	bigint	The last number of bytes in the database log used by the query plan within the aggregation interval. Applies **only to Azure SQL Database**
min_log_bytes_used	bigint	The minimum number of bytes in the database log used by the query plan within the aggregation interval. Applies **only to Azure SQL Database**
max_log_bytes_used	bigint	The maximum number of bytes in the database log used by the query plan within the aggregation interval. Applies **only to Azure SQL Database**
stdev_log_bytes_used	float	The standard deviation number of bytes in the database log used by the query plan within the aggregation interval Applies **only to Azure SQL Database**
avg_tempdb_space_used	float	Average amount of tempdb space used by the query
last_tempdb_space_used	bigint	The last amount of tempdb space used by the query plan within the aggregation interval
min_tempdb_space_used	bigint	Minimum amount of tempdb space used by the query plan within the aggregation interval
max_tempdb_space_used	bigint	Maximum amount of tempdb space used by the query plan within the aggregation interval
stdev_tempdb_space_used	float	The standard deviation of tempdb space used by the query plan within the aggregation interval

sys.query_store_runtime_stats_interval

The sys.query_store_runtime_stats_interval catalog view is the most basic and smallest. It contains the start and end time of each runtime interval. Statistics collection intervals are in 1 minute, 5 minutes, 10 minutes, 15 minutes, 30 minutes, 1 hour, and 1-day segments. See more in Chapter 3 on how to configure this setting. Table 5-9 shows all the column names, data types, and descriptions for the columns in the sys.query_store_runtime_stats_interval catalog view.

Table 5-9. *Column listing and descriptions for sys.query_runtime_stats_interval*

Column name	Data type	Description
runtime_stats_interval_id	bigint	Primary key.
start_time	datetimeoffset	Start time of the interval.
end_time	datetimeoffset	End time of the interval.
comment	nvarchar(32)	Always NULL.

Conclusion

To get the most out of Query Store, you will need to understand how the catalog views are related to each other and query them directly for different use cases. All the information you need about what is running against your SQL Server is contained here depending on your settings and can be customized to your specifications. The data is here for the harvesting, and we looked at visual ways of looking at this data in Chapter 4 and will look at a stored procedure for retrieving data in Chapter 10.

CHAPTER 6

Query Store Use Cases

Query Store has different use cases that it is useful for. This chapter will go into detail on those use cases. We will discuss how to determine what is a normal workload on your database using Query Store by looking at the reports or catalog views and viewing changes against that baseline. Baselining a database is an essential skill for any DBA, and Query Store is a tool you can use to provide you with a baseline for your database. Sometimes you will need to identify what happened during a previous window of time. As a DBA you also will have to troubleshoot poorly performing queries or queries that have regressed in performance, and Query Store gives you the data to be able to do that as well. Query Store can help you identify the top consuming queries so you can see how to improve performance on the SQL Server database. Query Store can be used to capture queries after an upgrade of SQL Server to a different version and change the compatibility mode on each database later and fix any regressed queries, stabilizing upgrades of your SQL Server databases. Finally, we will look at how Query Store is used to track ad-hoc workloads and improve their performance.

Determining What Is a Normal Workload

With Query Store turned on, you are collecting data in the INTERVAL_LENGTH_MINUTES specified when you configured Query Store as discussed in Chapter 3. To refresh your memory on this configuration option, the data can be aggregated in 1, 5, 10, 15, 60, and 1440 minute intervals. With these data points in mind, you can let your normal workload run against your server and view the reports discussed in Chapter 4 starting with the Overall Resource Consumption Report as seen in Figure 6-1.

© Tracy Boggiano and Grant Fritchey 2019
T. Boggiano and G. Fritchey, *Query Store for SQL Server 2019*, https://doi.org/10.1007/978-1-4842-5004-4_6

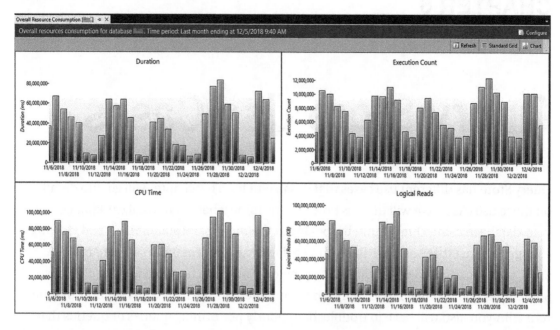

Figure 6-1. *Overall Resource Consumption report*

From viewing this report, you can determine what a normal workload is for your database. From the report in Figure 6-1, you will notice a pattern of 2 days a week where activity is low. Those happen to correspond to weekends which can tell us that this database is used in a company where less activity occurs on the weekends and most activity occurs on weekdays. We can also notice a pattern, where the duration is higher than normal, and logical reads are higher than in other periods. For those you want to click on those bars and drill down to the Top Resource Consuming Queries Report, we discussed in Chapter 4 to diagnose which queries caused those unusual patterns and determine if those workloads are something you need to be concerned about.

Another way to get to data is to query the catalog views discussed in Chapter 5. The query in Listing 6-1 queries data from the catalog views for the last 10 days and pulls the top 10 queries by duration.

Listing 6-1. T-SQL to top queries by duration in last 10 days

```
SELECT TOP 10 qt.query_sql_text,
     q.query_id,
     so.name,
     so.type,
```

```
        SUM(rs.count_executions * rs.avg_duration)
            AS 'Total Duration'
FROM sys.query_store_query_text qt
     INNER JOIN sys.query_store_query q
            ON qt.query_text_id = q.query_text_id
     INNER JOIN sys.query_store_plan p
            ON q.query_id = p.query_id
     INNER JOIN sys.query_store_runtime_stats rs
            ON p.plan_id = rs.plan_id
     INNER JOIN sys.query_store_runtime_stats_interval rsi
            ON rsi.runtime_stats_interval_id =
                    rs.runtime_stats_interval_id
     INNER JOIN sysobjects so on so.id = q.object_id
WHERE rsi.start_time >= DATEADD(DAY, -10, GETUTCDATE())
GROUP BY qt.query_sql_text,
     q.query_id,
     so.name,
     so.type
ORDER BY SUM(rs.count_executions * rs.avg_duration_time) DESC
```

Note   All times are stored in UTC time so you would need to adjust the query to fit your time zone for data to exactly match your time zone.

Establishing a Baseline for Queries

Query Store gives you the ability to establish a baseline for the queries in your database. Query Store stores all the execution runtime statistics in the catalog view sys.query_store_runtime_stats so you can query this catalog view to see a number of statistics about how your queries have performed in the past and are currently performing as you work to establish a baseline to compare against. It is not how you would baseline your server.

What Is a Baseline?

First, let's discuss what a baseline is. A baseline is a workload you run against your server that sets a starting point for comparisons against future runs of the same workload. In theory, you would run your workload to make any necessary changes to your environment; the changes could be code or hardware changes, and you would rerun the same workload and compare and see what metrics have changed.

How to Create a Baseline with Query Store

Establishing a baseline in Query Store involves knowing what data is being collected and when. When you look at the Overall Resource Consumption Report seen in Figure 6-1, it can be helpful to clear Query Store before starting your workload to establish your baseline. Two ways to do this were discussed in Chapter 3. One is to right-click on the database, go to Properties, then the Query Store tab. As seen in Figure 6-2, there is Purge Query Data that will clear all the data from Query Store so you can start your baseline. Be sure before you run your workload that your statistics collection interval is low enough to collect your data and you don't have to wait too long between each interval to run this next workload.

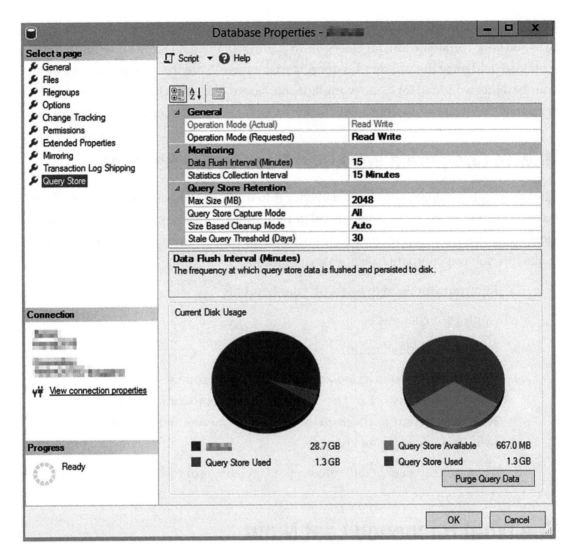

Figure 6-2. *Database properties for Query Store*

The second is to run the stored procedure in Listing 6-2.

Listing 6-2. Store procedure to clear all the data out of Query Store

```
USE [<Database>]
GO
EXEC sys.sp_query_store_flush_db;
```

Now we have a clean slate to capture data for our workload. To capture your workload so that you can replay it later, open SQL Server Profiler and pick the

137

TSQL_Replay template and create a server-side trace as we discussed in Chapter 1. Now run your workload, and let Query Store capture all the data for the queries in the workload, and once the workload is done, stop the trace. Note the time period you ran your baseline workload for future comparisons. Now make your changes to the code or server that you want to compare. See the next section on how to compare the results.

How to Compare a Workload Back to the Baseline

The best way to compare your workload back is to use the reports from Chapter 4. If you have set your statistics collection interval to 15 minutes, for example, you can run your workload outside the next interval to collect data for your comparison. The basic steps to make sure you can compare baselines are as follows:

1. Run your workload to establish your baseline.

2. Apply your changes.

3. Run your workload again.

4. Compare the results by looking at the Overall Resource Consumption Report and drilling down to the Top Consuming Resources Report to check on the particular queries that may have been impacted by your changes.

5. Then you can decide rather to keep your changes or roll them back.

See What Happened Last Night

A common problem is to have someone come over to you and say such and such ran slow yesterday at 5 AM and without any tracing turned you would have no idea what had run. Now with Query Store, all the queries that ran are being recorded for you to be able to see what ran yesterday at any time. By looking at the Top Consuming Resources Report, you can drill down to a specific time period and look for what was running slow. Not only can you tell what was running slow you could see what query caused a CPU spike or a large number of reads if someone had complained that the SAN had slowed down. Figure 6-3 shows your configuration options for narrowing down what happened on the server during the time frame you need and by the metric you heard was the problem.

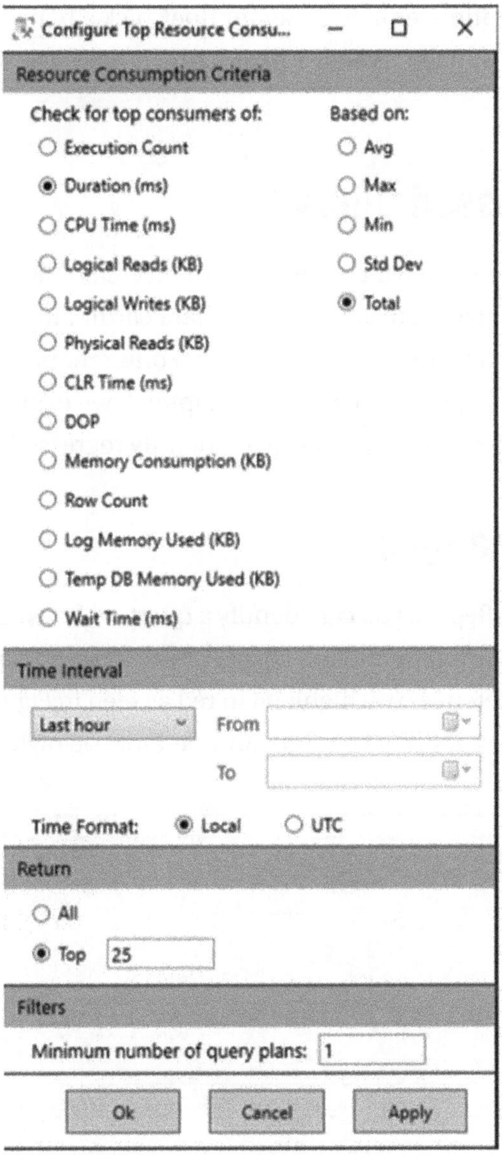

Figure 6-3. *Top Consuming Resources report configuration screen*

Troubleshooting Regressed Queries

One of the most powerful use cases for Query Store is to be able to identify queries that have regressed in performance. Queries can regress in performance for various reasons such as a change in statistics, the data cardinality has changed, indexes have been created, indexes that existed before could have been altered or deleted, etc. In

139

most cases, the Query Optimizer in SQL Server does pick a better plan, but there are times where it does not, and Query Store gives a quick, easy way to go in and find those queries.

What Is a Regressed Query?

A regressed query is a query in which the performance has changed due to a change on the system such as a change in statistics, the data cardinality has changed, indexes that have been created, etc. The change results in a different plan being generated than before that does not perform as well. Back in Chapter 4, we explored the Regressed Queries Report which gives you a quick way to identify regressed queries.

Viewing Plan Changes

In the Regressed Queries Report, you can identify a query with two plans and use the compare plan button at the top right-hand corner after you select both plans in the top right-hand pane. The differences will highlight in red as seen in Figure 6-4. And in Figure 6-5, you can see what difference there is between any operator you hightlight in the plans.

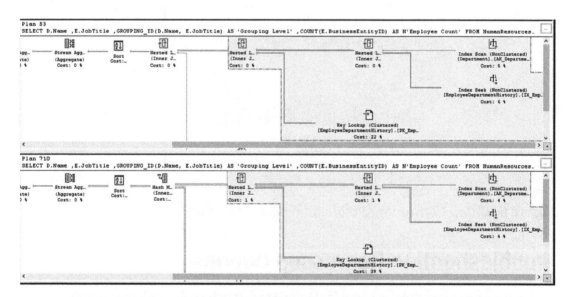

Figure 6-4. *Regressed Query peport comparing plan operator differences*

The differences seen in Figure 4-24 have a not equal sign highlighted in yellow.

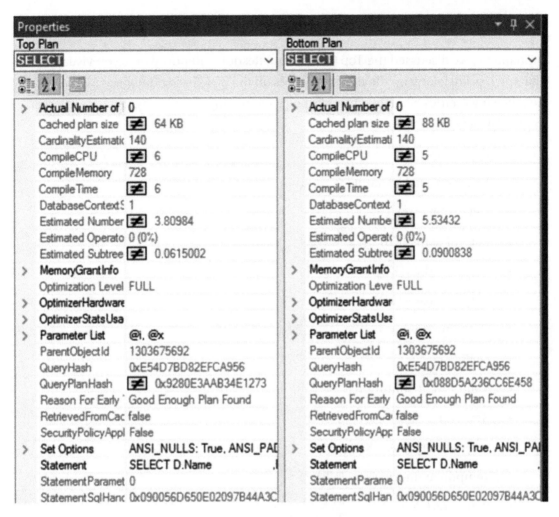

Figure 6-5. *Regressed Query report comparing report details*

As we have seen in Chapter 4, when viewing a query with multiple plans, you can force the plan manually from the report screen. If you find a plan that needs to be forced, you can force the plan from the report and monitor performance.

Identify Top Consuming Resource Queries

In Chapter 4, we discussed the Top Consuming Resource Report where you visually see what queries are taking up the most resources on the SQL Server database. We can view the following metrics when troubleshooting what the top consuming resource queries on the SQL Server database are:

- Execution count
- Duration (ms) (default)
- CPU Time (ms)
- Logical reads (KB)
- Logical writes (KB)
- Physical reads (KB)
- CLR time (ms)
- DOP
- Memory consumption (KB)
- Row count
- Log memory used (KB)
- Tempdb memory usage (KB)
- Wait time (ms)

They can be aggregated into totals, averages, minimums, maximums, and standard deviation. When looking for top consumers, total is a good starting place. If you are seeing high CPU, start with looking at the total with CPU time. The report will display by default the top 25 queries with their plans. You can then see if there is anything that could be tuned in those queries or perhaps a plan that can be forced.

Stabilizing SQL Server Upgrades

Another great benefit of Query Store is to help stabilize SQL Server upgrades. Every SQL Server upgrade due to changes to the query optimizer has the potential to cause regression in queries if you change the compatibility mode of a database. Since it is recommended best practice to change the compatibility mode of a database when you upgrade SQL Server so you can take advantage of the query optimizer enhancements and new T-SQL functions, it becomes even more critical to be able to stabilize the upgrade of SQL Server. Also, SQL Server 2014 introduced significant changes to the cardinality estimator causing some regressed queries when changing the compatibility mode.

Changing Compatibility Mode Effects

Before SQL Server 2014, changing compatibility modes didn't affect the query optimizer because compatibility mode did not affect the cardinality estimator because there had not been a new one released since SQL Server 7.0. So the only benefits you got form changing compatibility modes were any enhancements made to the query optimizer and new T-SQL functions.

Cardinality Estimation Changes Explained

Starting with the release of SQL Server 2014, Microsoft started making changes to the cardinality estimator (CE) which affects how queries estimate how many rows are being returned by the query. In most cases, the queries ran faster under the new CE, but some queries had some significant regressions. Your only recourse was to revert the compatibility mode or use trace flags to control the behavior.

In SQL Server 2016, Microsoft introduced database scoped configurations that allowed you to control MAXDOP, LEGACY_CARDINALITY ESTIMATION, PARAMETER_ SNIFFING, and QUERY_OPTIMIZER_HOTFIXES at the database level. The two most important ones in this list for what we are talking about are LEGACY_CARDINALITY ESTIMATION and QUERY_OPTIMIZER_HOTFIXES. If you set the LEGACY_ CARDINALITY ESTIMATION, it will use the old CE no matter what compatibility level the databases is set to. The advantage to this is you can still get to use the new T-SQL functions in the database and not have the query regressions. The QUERY_OPTIMIZER_ HOTFIXES option is the same thing as setting the trace flag 4199 which activates the all the query optimizer fixes put in the engine via a new version or patch or CU. Before 2016, you had to set trace flag 4199, and it applied to all the databases, and you had no easy way to troubleshoot and fix regressed queries.

Process for Testing and Completing Upgrades Using Query Store

Now that you are familiar with how changing the compatibility mode effects the query optimizer and CE and what may cause you regressed queries, let's talk about how to upgrade SQL Server the most effective way using Query Store to stabilize any regressed queries after the upgrade. This is best illustrated in Figure 6-6.

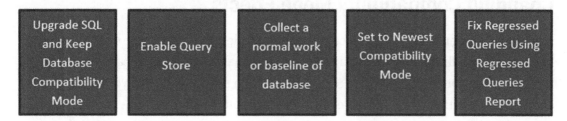

Figure 6-6. *Steps to upgrade SQL Server using Query Store*

The first step is to upgrade to SQL Server 2016 or higher. Next, you would enable Query Store on your database(s). Let your workload run on the database(s) as long as you think is necessary to capture a good baseline of your workload. Then set the compatibility mode to the newest mode on the database(s). Finally, monitor the Regressed Queries report discussed in Chapter 4 for plans that you need to force due to regression. Chapter 7 covers Automatic Plan Correction where starting in SQL Server 2017, Query Store will automatically force plans for you. See Chapter 7 for more details.

Finding and Improving Ad-hoc Workloads

Finally, Query Store can be used to find your ad-hoc queries and improve them. If you have a lot of ad-hoc queries, when you look at the Top Consuming Resources report, you will not see a large number of resources being consumed by queries with execution counts greater than one. If your systems are mostly ad-hoc workloads, it will not be ideal for working with Query Store as you are sending in different queries, and it is not able to aggregate data for you or force plans to help performance. While your application is generating ad-hoc queries, SQL Server is spending its time compiling queries for every new query that is executed, bloating the plan cache and consuming resources extra than if they were already in the plan cache. This will also cause bloat of Query Store because it will be storing different plans and aggregated rows of runtime statistics for each query.

This will cause the background processes that clean up Query Store to take up more resources as well to keep the space at a level where it can add data.

Instead, of using the Top Consuming Resources report, there is T-SQL you can run to first get the total number of query texts, queries, and plans, and then compare the query_hash and query_plan_hash to find your ad-hoc queries that are similar as seen in Listing 6-3.

Listing 6-3. T-SQL to check for ad-hoc workload

```
--Total Query Texts
SELECT COUNT(*) AS CountQueryTextRows
FROM sys.query_store_query_text;

--Total Queries
SELECT COUNT(*) AS CountQueryRows
FROM sys.query_store_query;

--Total distinct query hashes (different queries)
SELECT COUNT(DISTINCT query_hash) AS CountDifferentQueryRows
FROM  sys.query_store_query;

--Total plans
SELECT COUNT(*) AS CountPlanRows
FROM sys.query_store_plan;

--Total unique query_plan_hash (different plans)
SELECT COUNT(DISTINCT query_plan_hash) AS CountDifferentPlanRows
FROM sys.query_store_plan;
```

If you see a difference in CountQueryRows and CountDifferentQueryRows or CountPlanRows and CountDifferentPlansRows, that is an indication you have similar queries running, and you would benefit from writing them in a parameterized way such as in stored procedures if you can control the application code, so it can be compiled once and stored in memory and stored efficiently in Query Store. If you cannot manage the application code, you can have two other options. One is to use plan guides; a template for a plan guide is in Listing 6-4.

Listing 6-4. Template for implementing a plan guide for PARAMETERIZATION FORCED

```
DECLARE @stmt nvarchar(max);
DECLARE @params nvarchar(max);

EXEC sp_get_query_template
    N'<your query text goes here>',
    @stmt OUTPUT,
    @params OUTPUT;

EXEC sp_create_plan_guide
    N'TemplateGuide1',
    @stmt,
    N'TEMPLATE',
    NULL,
    @params,
    N'OPTION (PARAMETERIZATION FORCED)';
```

Alternately you can turn on PARAMETERIZATION FORCED at the database level using Listing 6-5.

Listing 6-5. Turn on PARATERIZATION FORCED at database level

```
ALTER DATABASE <database name> SET PARAMETERIZATION FORCED;
```

If in Listing 6-3 the counts remained close to the same, then you will not want to turn on PARAMETERIZATION FORCED. Instead, you will want to enable optimize for ad hoc workloads and set the QUERY_CAPTURE_MODE to AUTO for Query Store instead of ALL. See Listing 6-6 to set these options. This will keep the plans from bloating the plan cache because the first time a query is executed it will only store a stub and store the plan on the second execution for future reuse. The AUTO capture mode will let Query Store not capture these queries that consumed insignificant amount of resources to limit the amount that is stored.

Listing 6-6. Enable optimize for ad-hoc workloads and set capture mode to AUTO for Query Store

```
EXEC sys.sp_configure N'show advanced options', N'1'
GO
RECONFIGURE WITH OVERRIDE
GO
EXEC sys.sp_configure N'optimize for ad hoc workloads', N'1'
GO
RECONFIGURE WITH OVERRIDE
GO

ALTER DATABASE [QueryStoreTest] SET QUERY_STORE CLEAR;

ALTER DATABASE [QueryStoreTest] SET QUERY_STORE = ON
    (OPERATION_MODE = READ_WRITE, QUERY_CAPTURE_MODE = AUTO);
```

Conclusion

In this chapter, we explored several use cases for Query Store. We discussed how to establish a baseline so you can discover how your system normally performs and see what happens when you make changes. Then we discussed who to view what happened last night or any previous point in time for a problem. Next we discussed what regressed queries were and how to troubleshoot them and force plans. Then we discussed identifying top consuming queries so you could look at improving them. Next we looked at how you could use Query Store to stabilize the upgrade of SQL Server and why this is an important feature to use for this. Finally, we discussed who to use Query Store to improve your ad-hoc workloads.

CHAPTER 7

Forcing Plans

While the information collected in the Query Store and all that it tells you about the performance of your system is the part of Query Store that you'll use more frequently, the most powerful part of Query Store is the ability to force execution plans. Plan forcing is where the choices made by the optimizer during a compile or recompile event are superceded by a plan you select. Query Store provides enough information between the performance metrics and the execution plan to enable you to decide that, under some circumstances, you can pick a superior execution plan.

This chapter will show you how to use Query Store information and reports to identify a poorly behaving execution plan. With a badly behaving plan identified, we'll explore how to use the information in Query Store to identify a well-behaved plan, if one exists. With this information in hand, we can then force the good plan to be used.

Identifying Badly Behaved Execution Plans

Execution plans, also called query plans or show plans, are your window into the choices made by the query optimization process. They show how your T-SQL, indexes, statistics, tables, columns, and constraints make up your database, and its queries will be used to retrieve or modify the data stored there. Reading execution plans is a very dense topic. For a detailed look, you should read the book *Execution Plans* by Grant Fritchey (one of the co-authors of this book). Here we'll explore the information and reports that may suggest you have a poorly performing query. We'll then use that to lead us to an execution plan. We'll cover a few of the guideposts that can help you tell that a plan might not be supporting a query well, but we won't be covering all the details of how to read an execution plan.

To get started, we have to understand how we can use Query Store to identify a query that has both changed its execution plan and how that plan caused performance

T. Boggiano and G. Fritchey, *Query Store for SQL Server 2019*, https://doi.org/10.1007/978-1-4842-5004-4_7

to degrade. Another way you can identify poorly performing queries is when you get alerted to issues from the consumers of your database that performance is poor but with the information in the Query Store, we can be more proactive than that.

Identifying Regressed Queries

A regression is something that occurs when a query was behaving well and now performs poorly. You may have a query that runs badly from the start. These are easily identified and dealt with. You may have a query that slowly degrades in performance over time as more and more data is added to the system. These are also easily identified and dealt with. The real issues come when you have queries that were performing well and suddenly, sometimes intermittently, run slowly. Prior to Query Store, these were frequently difficult problems to solve.

The causes for these regressions are varied. You might see them when you migrate from earlier versions of SQL Server to later versions of SQL Server. These are caused by changes to how the query optimizer works and the introduction in SQL Server 2014 of a new cardinality estimation engine. You may see a regression caused by statistics on your database being incorrect or out of date. You could also be suffering from a problem known as bad parameter sniffing.

While incorrect and out-of-date statistics are probably the most common cause of regressions in query performance, the most talked about problem, and the one we'll use for our examples in this chapter, is bad parameter sniffing. Let's start by explaining what parameter sniffing is and how it can sometimes cause problems.

When you have a parameterized query, whether that's a stored procedure, a parameterized query from an ORM tool such as Entity Framework, or parameters in sp_executesql, the query optimizer will use the values passed to that parameter when compiling an execution plan. It takes those exact values and uses them to look at the statistics for the column or index being referenced and creates and execution plan based on those precise values. This sampling of values is what is known as parameter sniffing. The majority of the time, this is a benign practice. A lot of the time, this is a very helpful practice. Sometimes though, you'll see a situation where a plan gets created for one value that performs well enough for the query immediately called. However, all other queries perform very poorly with that same execution plan. This situation is known as bad parameter sniffing.

When you hit a situation where a query was performing well, but is suddenly performing poorly, you can use the information in Query Store to identify both the query metrics that define the performance and get a look at the execution plans both for when the query was running well and when it was running badly. You can do this one of two ways. You can run T-SQL code against the data collected in Query Store. Alternatively, you can use the Regressed Query report. Since the Regressed Query report may not always identify a query that is giving you problems as a regressed query, it's a very good idea to know how to retrieve this information from the Query Store data yourself.

Identifying Regressed Queries from Query Store Data

We discussed the information collected by the Query Store in Chapter 2. We then went over the basics of how to retrieve data from the Query Store catalog views in Chapter 5. If you don't get what we're doing with the queries below, I'd recommend going back and reviewing those chapters before proceeding with this one.

To start with, we need a query that we can reliably get different execution plans from. The data distribution in the Person.Address table is such that depending on what value is used to filter the City column, you can get a couple of different execution plans in the AdventureWorks database. Here is the query we'll use to explore behavior in the rest of the chapter:

```
CREATE OR ALTER PROC [dbo].[AddressByCity] @City NVARCHAR(30)
AS
    SELECT a.AddressID,
        a.AddressLine1,
        a.AddressLine2,
        a.City,
        sp.Name AS StateProvinceName,
        a.PostalCode
    FROM Person.Address AS a
    JOIN Person.StateProvince AS sp
        ON a.StateProvinceID = sp.StateProvinceID
    WHERE a.City = @City;
GO
```

With this procedure in place, we can execute the query with one of two different values to arrive at two different execution plans. If you run the following script with execution plans enabled, you can see the two plans. Note: For test purposes we're using a simple way to clear the procedure cache. This may not be the best approach on a production system:

```
EXEC dbo.AddressByCity @City = N'London';

ALTER DATABASE SCOPED CONFIGURATION CLEAR PROCEDURE_CACHE;

EXEC dbo.AddressByCity @City = N'Mentor';
```

This is a classic case of parameter sniffing resulting in different execution plans. Each plan is optimized for the result set it is returning; 434 rows for the value "London" and one row for the value "Mentor." However, each plan causes poor performance for the opposite data set. What I mean here is that the plan to return 434 rows runs fast when returning 434 rows, but it doesn't run as fast as the other plan when returning only a few rows. The opposite is also true. In fact, the query will run so much slower when using the plan for "Mentor" when returning 434 rows that it will be marked as a regressed query in the Regressed Query report.

Regressed Query Report

We're going to be covering the reports in detail in Chapter 4. However, here we want to show how the behavior of the dbo.AddressByCity procedure returns in the report:

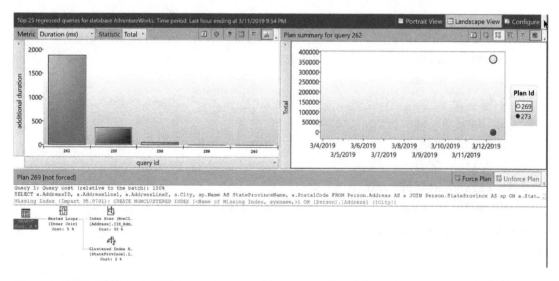

Figure 7-1. *Regressed Query report showing poor performance*

The first pane, on the left, is a listing of the queries based on the metric you're measuring (duration by default). The second pane in the report shows query execution speed and the different plans involved. Clicking on one of the dots will change the plan being displayed in the bottom pane. Hovering over the dot will show how many executions it represents, average runtime, and more. Again, for more details on using the reports, see Chapter 4.

You can't simply run the code above and arrive at a regressed query. The Regressed Query report compares behavior over time. So to get the report to generate, you have to run the code multiple times over a period of time. To simulate this yourself, you can run the following script. You may have to run it multiple times to get the query to show up as a regressed query because it has to have the data inside the Query Store to get the report to fire and it has to show a substantial difference over time. However, this script will work:

```
--Establish baseline behavior
EXEC dbo.AddressByCity @City = N'London';
GO 100

--Remove the plan from cache
ALTER DATABASE SCOPED CONFIGURATION CLEAR PROCEDURE_CACHE;
--Compile a new plan
EXEC dbo.AddressByCity @City = N'Mentor';
GO

--Execute the code to show query regression
EXEC dbo.AddressByCity @City = N'London';
GO 100
```

You should be able to see the query in the Regressed Query report and it should show two different execution plans the same as Figure 7-1.

Warning Signs in Execution Plans

Regressed query behavior is driven by changes to the execution plans. There isn't room in this book to cover everything you need to know to read execution plans. For a detailed examination on that topic, we recommend Grant Fritchey's book, *SQL Server Execution Plans* (Redgate Press, 2018). However, there a few warning signs we can look for in execution plans as a quick set of guides. Just understand, these will only guide you initially. You'll have to eventually learn the details to read and understand the information inside execution plans.

Here is a core set of things to look at when examining execution plans for the first time.

First Operator: A detailed collection of information about the plan itself

Most Costly Operator: The highest estimated cost showing a highly likely culprit for poor performance

Warnings and Errors: Issues experienced by the optimization process, if any

Fat Pipes: An indication of data flow, with wider pipes showing more data

Scans: An indicator of larger data movement

Extra Operators: Operators that you can't explain readily why they are there or what they are doing

Estimates vs. Actuals: The comparisons between the estimated number of rows or executions for an operator and the actual number of either

Here's what you are using these guides to look for. I'll use the execution plan that is causing us the most trouble, the one from the value of "Mentor" as shown here in Figure 7-2:

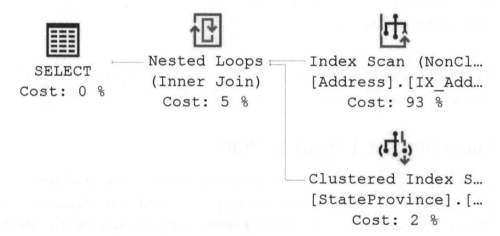

Figure 7-2. *Execution plan for the value "Mentor"*

We'll now walk through the guideposts looking for information about this plan.

First Operator

The first operator is the one all the way on the left side of any plan. It will usually be
labeled by the type of operation your T-SQL is performing: SELECT, INSERT, UPDATE,
and DELETE. Right-click on that operator and select properties. You'll see something like
Figure 7-3:

Cached plan size	32 KB
CardinalityEstimationModelVersion	140
CompileCPU	78
CompileMemory	424
CompileTime	106
DatabaseContextSettingsId	1
Estimated Number of Rows	1.66667
Estimated Operator Cost	0 (0%)
Estimated Subtree Cost	0.193771
MemoryGrantInfo	
MissingIndexes	
Optimization Level	FULL
OptimizerHardwareDependentProperties	
OptimizerStatsUsage	
Parameter List	@City
Column	@City
Parameter Compiled Value	N'Mentor'
Parameter Data Type	nvarchar(30)
ParentObjectId	1271675578
QueryHash	0xDD75E124763781F2
QueryPlanHash	0x84AED2D3F83C43D2
Reason For Early Termination Of Statement Optir	Good Enough Plan Found

Figure 7-3. *Partial list of first operator properties*

This is only a partial of all the properties and information exposed through the
first operator of an execution plan. When looking at plan regressions, chances are high
that you **may** be seeing problems caused by changes in data or statistics, or parameter
sniffing. In that case, the Parameter List property shows you the parameter or parameters
used to compile the execution plan. You can see in Figure 7-3 that this plan used the
value "Mentor."

Most Costly Operator

The plan shown in Figure 7-2 is very simple and easy to read. You can quickly spot that the Index Scan operator is 93% of the estimated cost. These costs are based on calculations within the optimizer and are not reflective of actual behavior. However, since the numbers that drive the costs are derived from your code, objects, and the row counts in the statistics, it's a value we use to examine execution plans. A high cost operator may indicate where the problem lies.

Warnings and Errors

These will show as a yellow caution sign or a red "X". They can be indicators of problems with the code that affect how the execution plan behaves. There are none in Figure 7-2.

Fat Pipes

The arrows that connect the operators represent data flow. Big pipes reflect a lot of data flow, whereas small pipes represent small data flow. Look for the fat pipes to understand how data is being moved. You also have to look for transitions where more and more data is created, or where data is moved from disk and then filtered later. These can be strong indicators of problems.

Scans

A scan indicates that the entire table or index was read in order to retrieve data. This is not necessarily a problem; however, it indicates possible large amounts of I/O and therefore is something to consider when evaluating an execution plan. Please note that seeks, the opposite of scans, can also cause problems depending on the rest of the plan. Index scans such as the one in Figure 7-2 should lead us to question the plan. We have a data set that is filtering down to one row yet it's scanning an entire clustered index to do that.

Extra Operators

This concept is a little harder to explain. If you're looking at a plan and you can't explain what an operator is, or why a given operator is being used, that should draw your eye for consideration. Let's take a look at the plan for the value "London" in Figure 7-4:

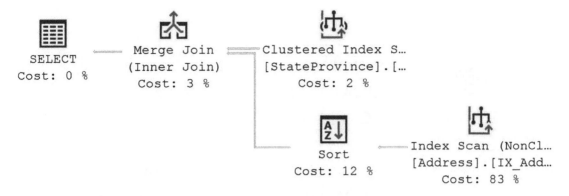

Figure 7-4. *Execution plan for the value "London"*

In this plan we have an Index Scan, a Clustered Index Scan, a Merge Join, and a Sort. When you consider the query in dbo.AddressByCity, you'll note that there is no ORDER BY command. Therefore, in this case, the Sort operator is a mystery, an extra operator. Why do we have a Sort operation? The answer here is because the optimizer decided that the Merge Join was faster for the larger data set. However, a Merge Join requires that all data be ordered. So a Sort operator was added to satisfy the needs of the Merge Join.

Estimated vs. Actual

You can only compare these values when you're looking at an Actual plan, which looks like the same thing as an Estimated plan but has additional runtime metrics. In short, to capture an Actual plan, you have to execute the query. If we look at the execution plan for the value of "Mentor" after executing the query with the value of "London," we can see this comparison in action as shown in Figure 7-5:

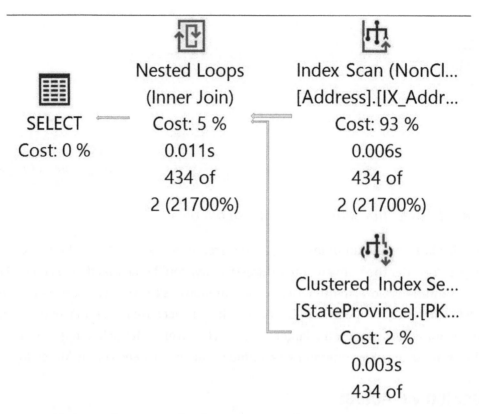

Figure 7-5. *Estimated vs. Actual values compared*

Here we're seeing one of the estimated vs. actual comparisons, the number of rows processed by each operator. You can see that the Nested Loops join processed 434 rows of the 2 that it anticipated. In this case, the estimated number of rows was 2, but the actual was 434. This wide disparity, 21,700%, can be an indicator for why performance is poor.

Even with these guides for looking at execution plans, you're still going to need to drill down into the properties in order to understand better how execution plans work. However, the guideposts will get you started. In order to evaluate if a plan is better, it's a good idea to learn how to compare one plan to the other.

Comparing Execution Plans

From the Regressed Query report (as well as other Query Store reports), you have the ability to easily, and quickly, compare execution plans. Yes, you can look at the plans graphically and compare them by clicking on the dots. However, there is a utility for comparing execution plans that shows a lot more detail and functionality.

To access this functionality, you'll need to shift-click on two of the execution plans (you can only compare two plans at a time). Then click on the toolbar of the report as shown in Figure 7-6:

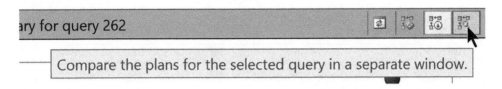

Figure 7-6. *The toolbar for comparing two execution plans*

When you click on this after selecting two plans, a new window will open looking like Figure 7-7:

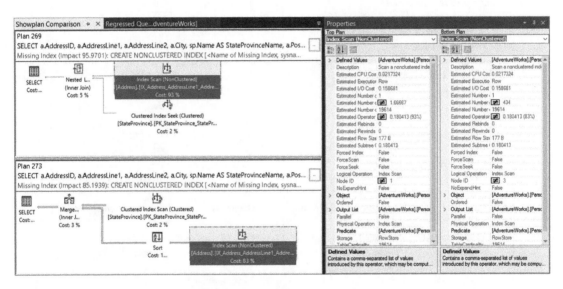

Figure 7-7. *Two execution plans being compared*

What you're seeing in Figure 7-7 are two execution plans being compared in the two panes, top and bottom, on the left. On the right are two sets of properties from a selected operator. Those property values are also being compared. The shading (pink in my case) around the operators in both plans is indicated operators, or even sets of operators, that are common between two plans. So, in our plan, the scan of the index on the Person. Address table is essentially the same in both plans. The other operators are different. This information can be used to help troubleshoot performance either by showing you a common problem needing a solution (in this case a scan of all the data in an index) or by showing you the differences in the plan that are causing poor performance.

Clicking on any operator on the left panes will change the property values on the right side, allowing you to further explore the details and differences. Figure 7-8 is the properties from the common Index Scan operator:

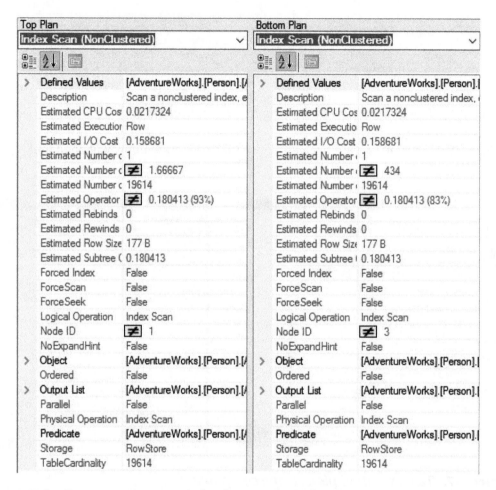

Figure 7-8. *Common operator in both execution plans*

The property values that do not match have the yellow "does not equal" icon in front of those values. You can see that overall, the estimated costs, row size, object information, and the rest are all the same. It's only the estimated number of rows, node ID, and the estimated operator percentage costs that are different. In fact, the percentage estimates are only different because all the other operators in the two plans are different.

Comparing common operators, especially in this case, a scan, can give you indications where the query performance may be improved by changes to the code or structure. However, the whole point of using plan forcing is to avoid having to modify the code or structure. You mainly want to compare plans so that you're sure the one you pick to force is more likely to succeed.

When you are looking at operators that are not marked as common between the two plans, in order to compare those operators, you would need to select each one individually. As a general rule, this won't tell you much about the plans because when different operators are performing different functions between plans, comparing them is of little use.

You combine the performance metrics, the wait statistics, and the information you glean from the execution plans in question. Along with this information, you should also take into account things like the importance of the query, the frequency at which it is being called, and other factors that will help you decide that, in fact, one of these plans will outperform the other for your most common needs.

Once you've decided which of the plans you want to force, you have several options to force the plan.

Forcing and Unforcing Execution Plans

When a plan regresses for whatever reason, the single best solution is to make changes, whether that is to code, structure, or statistics. However, it's just not always possible, or desirable, to make those changes. In this case, we're going to want to force a plan. There are several things you should know about plan forcing before we get on to how it's done.

Plan forcing overrides the work of the query optimizer. When you choose to force a plan, that is the plan that will always be used until you unforce, or invalidate, that plan. You can only force a plan that is valid for a given query. If you make changes to the code or the structures, such as dropping an index or something along those lines, it invalidates the plan, forcing is no longer possible.

The query optimizer will still generate a plan if one is not in the cache. However, in the event that you have a forced plan, any other plan generated by the optimizer will be discarded. You can sometimes see a situation where a forced plan looks different than the original plan that you forced. Because the optimizer still goes through the optimization process, if a plan that is morally equivalent (Microsoft's term) is generated, meaning a plan that for all intents and purposes is exactly the same, that morally equivalent plan will be used. However, in most cases, you'll see the exact plan that you chose to force.

SQL Server has long had a function that is similar in behavior to plan forcing in the Query Store, plan guides. These were a way to apply a query hint or even suggest an entire execution plan for a query, like plan forcing. However, they are very difficult to use and frequently fail. This is one of many reasons why plan forcing in Query Store is so attractive. If you are using plan guides, plan forcing overrides the plan guides. Although, you'll still see evidence that guide was applied in both Extended Events and the execution plan itself.

When you mark a plan as forced, that is stored within the Query Store catalog views. This means that plan forcing will survive a restart, a detach, or even a failover in a clustered environment. This is because the fact that a plan is forced has been persisted to disk with the database. The only way to stop plan forcing is to invalidate the plan as described earlier, or choose to stop forcing that plan.

Because data and statistics change over time, it's a good idea to plan to review forced plans on a regular basis. You want to be sure that the reasons for forcing a particular plan still hold true as things change over time. It's also a very good idea to be very judicious about plan forcing and only do it when absolutely necessary in order to address regression.

Forcing Plans Through the Reports

Choosing to force a plan is never difficult. It's especially easy inside the Query Store reports. In the right-hand pane where you can see the performance of the queries over time, you'll see the execution plans for a query. There may be one, or there may be several. In Figure 7-9 you can see that I have two. They are listed on the right of Figure 7-9 in the little box labeled "Plan ID":

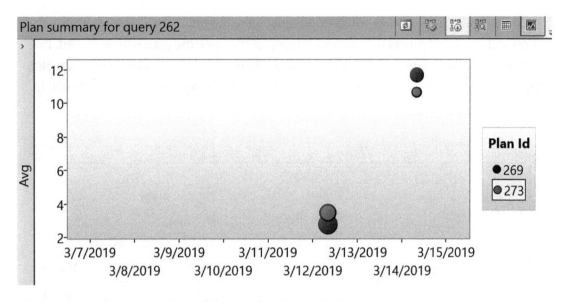

Figure 7-9. *Two execution plans in the Query Store report*

Once we decide which of the plans we wish to force, we just have to click on that Plan ID value on the right, either 269 or 273 in Figure 7-9. With that selected, the toolbar above has an icon for forcing plans as shown in Figure 7-10:

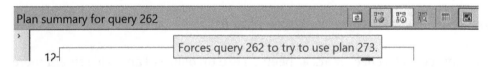

Figure 7-10. *Button in the report that lets you force plans*

Clicking that button opens a confirmation window. You have the opportunity to choose not to force the plan. Figure 7-11 shows the window:

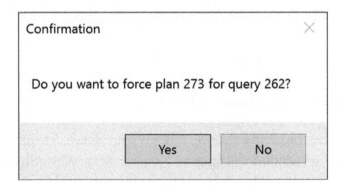

Figure 7-11. *Confirming that you wish to force a plan*

Clicking on the Yes button will immediately force the plan. Clicking on the No button will of course cancel the process. After you click yes, the plan will be forced. In my case, I'm choosing to force plan 273. When I do this, the report then marks that plan with a check mark. You can see this immediately in the Query Store report as shown in Figure 7-12:

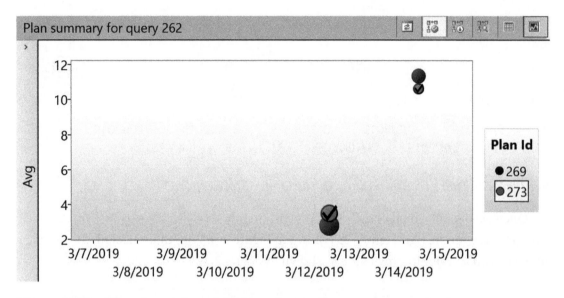

Figure 7-12. *The plans after picking a plan to force*

You can see that a check mark as been placed on plan 273 and will remain there until the plan forcing is removed. This is an immediate indication that the plan has been forced. You'll also see that the "Force Plan" button is marked as depressed when the plan is forced and not depressed when the plan is not forced.

Another way to force the plan is immediately below the pane we've been looking at in Figures 7-9 and 7-12. Another set of buttons are visible as shown in Figure 7-13:

Figure 7-13. *Plan forcing buttons in the Query Store report*

This button works the same as before. Pick the plan you wish to force and select the button. A confirmation window will open and you can acknowledge forcing the plan.

Choosing to remove forcing, or unforcing a plan, is very simple. You have to use the button shown in Figure 7-13. When you have a plan selected that has already been forced, the "Unforce Plan" button will be enabled. You can then remove plan forcing for that query. You'll again be prompted to confirm that you are unforcing the plan.

Forcing Plans Using T-SQL

You can also force a plan programmatically using T-SQL. The actual functionality of plan forcing through T-SQL is extremely easy. The only trick is that you have to have two pieces of information. You have to have the query_id within the Query Store and you have to have the plan_id. As you can see above, you can retrieve these using the Query Store reports. You can also use T-SQL against the Query Store catalog views as outlined in Chapter 5. With T-SQL you can retrieve the query_id and plan_id. With those in hand, forcing the plan is quite simple:

```
EXEC sys.sp_query_store_force_plan 262,273;
```

Since we're now doing this programmatically, there is no confirmation necessary. Assuming that both ID values are accurate and that the plan chosen is a valid plan, the plan_id, in this case 273, is forced for the query_id, in this case 262. If either ID is invalid, you'll get an error.

Choosing to unforce the plan programmatically is not very difficult either:

```
EXEC sys.sp_query_store_unforce_plan 262,273;
```

Again, there is no confirmation needed when forcing and unforcing programmatically through T-SQL.

Determining Which Plans Have Been Forced

As you've seen in Figure 7-12, it's very easy to see if a plan has been forced. There is even a report that lists forced plans. We'll go over that report in Chapter 4 in some detail. The question should be, is there a way to programmatically tell that a plan has been forced. The answer to this is, of course, yes. You just have to query the Query Store catalog views:

```
SELECT qsq.query_id,
       qsp.plan_id,
       qsp.is_forced_plan
```

```
FROM sys.query_store_query AS qsq
    JOIN sys.query_store_plan AS qsp
        ON qsp.query_id = qsq.query_id
WHERE qsq.query_id = 262;
```

The results of this query look like Figure 7-14:

	query_id	plan_id	is_forced_plan
1	262	269	0
2	262	273	1

Figure 7-14. *Showing which query plan is forced programmatically*

You can quickly see that the plan_id 273 has been forced since it's `is_forced_plan` value is set to 1, while the other plan, 269, is not forced.

You can also see if a plan is forced by looking at some execution plans. You won't see it on plans where you just capture an estimated plan if the plan is not yet in cache. You won't see it on a plan from the Query Store itself. You will see this on pretty much any other plan. What you're looking for is a little obscure. We'll need to go the properties of the first operator and look for the "Use Plan" property value as shown in Figure 7-15:

StatementSqlHandle	0x09005BEBBF981
Use plan	True
WaitStats	

Figure 7-15. *The "Use Plan" property in the first operator*

This is only available as a property in the first operator. It's not visible in the tooltip. You'll only see this on a plan that has been forced. You won't even see the property on any other plan, so there is no "Use Plan" that will resolve to False.

Conclusion

Query regression is a real problem. The best way to solve it still remains modifying the code, structure, or statistics to ensure a more appropriate plan is generated. However, when you must, you do have the capability of forcing an execution plan. There are plenty of ways to keep an eye on plan forcing, so you can adjust them as necessary when the structure or code changes or other changes are made to the system that may affect plan generation. As already mentioned, only use this functionality when you have to and have a plan for a regular review of the queries that have forced plans.

CHAPTER 8

Auto Plan Correction and Wait Statistics

The information captured and stored within Query Store begins to open up new functionality for Microsoft and you. First, for Microsoft, having the ability to identify a query that has suffered from a regression (as we describe in Chapter 7) means that they can monitor the system and, using the information in the Query Store, automate forcing a plan to fix the regression. This is the Auto Plan Correction at work. Second, for us, the addition of wait statistics within the Query Store information opens up additional troubleshooting possibilities.

This chapter explores additional capabilities of Query Store including:

- The ability to automatically mark queries with regressions and the new catalog views that support this

- The capacity for SQL Server to automatically force, or unforce, a plan based on its performance regressing

- The 23 categories of wait statistics that have been added to the Query Store information

Automatic Plan Correction

The concepts of Automatic Plan Correction are completely built on Query Store. Without the information collected by Query Store, the ability of SQL Server and Azure SQL Database to determine that a plan has regressed would not be possible. Remember that the core of plan regression is built around the idea that the query itself has not changed. Changes in code cause changes in behavior all the time. It's when

© Tracy Boggiano and Grant Fritchey 2019
T. Boggiano and G. Fritchey, *Query Store for SQL Server 2019*, https://doi.org/10.1007/978-1-4842-5004-4_8

you don't change the code or the structure of the database and performance degrades anyway that you have a regression. Query Store makes identifying regressions easier.

With the regression identified, the basic approach of Automatic Plan Correction is simple. The behavior for this query was better under the older plan. SQL Server can, when Automatic Plan Correction is enabled, automatically force that older plan, the last known good plan. Then, the behavior of the system is observed again for a time. If forcing the last good plan didn't work, then it can be automatically unforced. All this occurs behind the scenes with no real input from the user, the developer, or the DBA.

This behavior makes the job of tuning SQL Server easier because instead of attempting to fix simple issues that can be readily automated, you have time to address more difficult subjects that require more knowledge and understanding. Simply picking the last well-behaved plan and applying it is simple tuning, but it can solve a large number of issues easily.

Identifying Regression

We can start by understanding how SQL Server identifies a regressed query and how it communicates why it thinks that query has regressed. Luckily, all this functionality is summarized in a new dynamic management view: sys.dm_db_tuning_ recommendations.

However, before we can show off the behavior of the new DMV, it's necessary to have a query which will reliably supply behavior that can be identified as a regression. In order to do that, we'll have to make some modifications to the standard AdventureWorks database. Adam Machanic has a script called BigAdventure that uses some of the tables from AdventureWorks to create a much larger database. The code is available to download here: `http://dataeducation.com/thinking-big-adventure/`. First run Adam's script to create the necessary structures. With that in place, we'll run this script to create a stored procedure and modify the database:

```
CREATE INDEX ix_ActualCost ON dbo.bigTransactionHistory (ActualCost);
GO

--a simple query for the experiment
CREATE OR ALTER PROCEDURE dbo.ProductByCost (@ActualCost MONEY)
AS
SELECT bth.ActualCost
```

```
FROM dbo.bigTransactionHistory AS bth
JOIN dbo.bigProduct AS p
ON p.ProductID = bth.ProductID
WHERE bth.ActualCost = @ActualCost;
GO

--ensuring that Query Store is on and has a clean data set
ALTER DATABASE AdventureWorks SET QUERY_STORE = ON;
ALTER DATABASE AdventureWorks SET QUERY_STORE CLEAR;
GO
```

All this is necessary to enable us to create a load with queries that will suffer from a regression in a reliable fashion. With these preparations in place, in order to see the regression occur, we'll run the following script:

```
-- 1. Establish a history of query performance
EXEC dbo.ProductByCost @ActualCost = 8.2205;
GO 30

-- 2. Remove the plan from cache
DECLARE @PlanHandle VARBINARY(64);
SELECT  @PlanHandle = deps.plan_handle
FROM    sys.dm_exec_procedure_stats AS deps
WHERE   deps.object_id = OBJECT_ID('dbo.ProductByCost');
IF @PlanHandle IS NOT NULL
    BEGIN
        DBCC FREEPROCCACHE(@PlanHandle);
    END
GO

-- 3. Execute a query that will result in a different plan
EXEC dbo.ProductByCost @ActualCost = 0.0;
GO

-- 4. Establish a new history of poor performance
EXEC dbo.ProductByCost @ActualCost = 8.2205;
GO 15
```

That script does a number of things. I've placed markers in the comments in the code so that we can refer back to each section of the code to understand what is happening. First, at number 1, we have to establish behavior for the query. It takes a number of executions to establish that a query is behaving a certain way, capturing the data in Query Store. Next, at number 2, we remove the plan from the plan cache by getting the plan_handle and using FREEPROCCACHE to remove just the one plan from cache. This means that the next execution will have to compile a new plan. Without this step, even if we executed the query with different values, the plan would remain the same until it naturally aged out of cache. By forcibly removing it from cache, we set up the next step. In step 3, we execute the query, but we use a different value which has a very different data distribution in the statistics. This results in a change to the execution plan. Finally, in step 4, we again establish a pattern of behavior with the new execution plan.

Before I explain why the performance was so bad between the two versions of the execution plan, let's quickly see if this resulted in a regression by querying sys.dm_db_tuning_recommendations like this:

```
SELECT ddtr.type,
       ddtr.reason,
       ddtr.last_refresh,
       ddtr.state,
       ddtr.score,
       ddtr.details
FROM sys.dm_db_tuning_recommendations AS ddtr;
```

The results should look like Figure 8-1:

Figure 8-1. *Results in the tuning recommendations DMV*

The reason for this is easy enough to understand. If we were to look at the execution plan generated the first time we executed the store procedure using the value 8.2205, it looks like this:

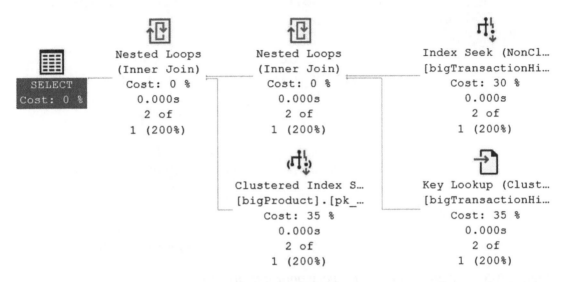

Figure 8-2.   *Original execution plan for dbo.ProductByCost stored procedure*

There could be tuning opportunities with this query as you can see in the plan with the Key Lookup operation. However, the plan works well enough for the data set being retrieved. The estimated number of rows was 1 and the actual was 2, which is extremely close, so the plan performs fairly well. After recompiling using the value 0.0, even when executed using the value 8.2205, the plan looks like this:

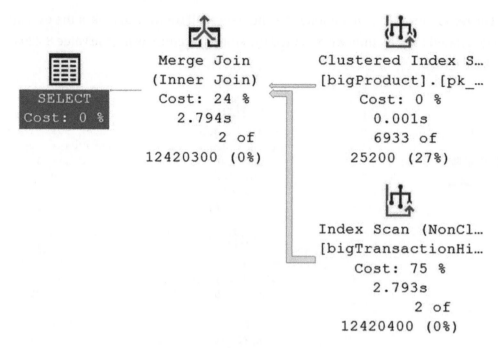

SELECT Cost: 0 %	Merge Join (Inner Join) Cost: 24 % 2.794s 2 of 12420300 (0%)
	Clustered Index S... [bigProduct].[pk_... Cost: 0 % 0.001s 6933 of 25200 (27%)
	Index Scan (NonCl... [bigTransactionHi... Cost: 75 % 2.793s 2 of 12420400 (0%)

Figure 8-3. *Execution plan with very poor performance*

The reason for this change is because the value 0.0 has 12,420,400 rows as shown in the plan, not the two we were dealing with originally. This different plan degraded performance seriously because we're scanning a giant index to retrieve only two rows rather than a simple seek. By executing the query multiple times, SQL Server was able to identify a regression and added data to sys.dm_db_tuning_recommendations. Let's take a closer look at that information in Figure 8-4:

	type	reason	last_refresh	state	score	details
1	FORCE_LAST_GOOD_PLAN	Average query CPU time changed from 0.16ms to 49...	2019-05-11 14:11:46.6866667	{"currentValue":"Active","reason":"AutomaticTuni...	36	{"planForceDetails":{"queryId":2,"regressedPlanI...

Figure 8-4. *Suggested tuning recommendations*

The first column tells us the type of tuning recommendation, in this case, FORCE_ LAST_GOOD_PLAN. Microsoft is likely to add further recommendations in the future. The next column is the reason for the recommendation and reads as follows:

Average query CPU time changed from 0.16ms to 4909.41ms

As we explained above, changing the execution plan to scan the index instead of seeking on it degraded performance. We executed the procedure enough times that averages were established and it went from 0.16ms to 4909.41ms on average, a huge leap.

The next column lets us know when the recommendation was last updated. Because things change within the system, you can, and will, see changes made to recommendations over time.

We also have the state column. This is JSON data showing us the current status of the recommendation as follows:

{"currentValue":"Active", "reason":"AutomaticTuningOptionNotEnabled"}

The recommendation is active, but it is not implemented. The reason for this is clear, we have yet to enable Automatic Tuning. Finally, all the details of the information are shown in another JSON column:

{"planForceDetails":{"queryId":2, "regressedPlanId":2, "regressedPlanExecutionCount":15, "regressedPlanErrorCount":0, "regressedPlanCpuTimeAverage":4.909411600000000e+006," regressedPlanCpuTimeStddev":1.181213221539555e+007, "recommendedPlanId": 1, "recommendedPlanExecutionCount":30, "recommendedPlanErrorCount": 0, "recommendedPlanCpuTimeAverage":1.622333333333333e+002, "recommended PlanCpuTimeStddev":2.380063281138177e+002}, "implementationDetails": {"method":"TSql", "script":"exec sp_query_store_force_plan @query_id = 2, @plan_id = 1"}}

That's very difficult to read, so we'll lay it out in a table to make it easier to see:

Table 8-1 list the columns in the JSON data in the details column above in the DMV.

Table 8-1. *Details of the tuning recommendation from the JSON data*

planForceDetails	
queryID	2: query_id value from the Query Store
regressedPlanID	2: The plan_id value from the Query Store of the problem plan
regressedPlanExecutionCount	5: Number of times the regressed plan was used
regressedPlanErrorCount	0: When there is a value, errors during execution
regressedPlanCpuTimeAverage	4.909411600000000e+006: Average CPU of the plan
regressedPlanCpuTimeStddev	1.181213221539555e+006: Standard deviation of that value
recommendedPlanID	1: The plan_id that the tuning recommendation is suggesting
recommendedPlanExecutionCount	30: Number of times the recommended plan was used
recommendedPlanErrorCount	0: When there is a value, errors during execution

(continued)

Table 8-1. (*continued*)

planForceDetails	
recommendedPlanCpuTimeAverage	1.622333333333333e+002: Average CPU of the plan
recommendedPlanCpuTimeStddev	2.380063281138177e+002: Standard deviation of that value
implementationDetails	
Method	TSql: Value will always be T-SQL until new types of recommendations are created
script	exec sp_query_store_force_plan @query_id = 2, @plan_id = 1

This data means that you don't need to enable Automatic Tuning in order to see what types of suggested changes are needed in your system. You can, if you want to, query this information much more directly by using JSON queries as follows:

```
WITH DbTuneRec
AS (SELECT ddtr.reason,
           ddtr.score,
           pfd.query_id,
           pfd.regressedPlanId,
           pfd.recommendedPlanId,
           JSON_VALUE(ddtr.state,
                      '$.currentValue') AS CurrentState,
           JSON_VALUE(ddtr.state,
                      '$.reason') AS CurrentStateReason,
           JSON_VALUE(ddtr.details,
                      '$.implementationDetails.script') AS
                      ImplementationScript
    FROM sys.dm_db_tuning_recommendations AS ddtr
       CROSS APPLY
       OPENJSON(ddtr.details,
               '$.planForceDetails')
       WITH (query_id INT '$.queryId',
             regressedPlanId INT '$.regressedPlanId',
             recommendedPlanId INT '$.recommendedPlanId') AS pfd)
```

```
SELECT qsq.query_id,
       dtr.reason,
       dtr.score,
       dtr.CurrentState,
       dtr.CurrentStateReason,
       qsqt.query_sql_text,
       CAST(rp.query_plan AS XML) AS RegressedPlan,
       CAST(sp.query_plan AS XML) AS SuggestedPlan,
       dtr.ImplementationScript
FROM DbTuneRec AS dtr
    JOIN sys.query_store_plan AS rp
        ON rp.query_id = dtr.query_id
            AND rp.plan_id = dtr.regressedPlanId
    JOIN sys.query_store_plan AS sp
        ON sp.query_id = dtr.query_id
            AND sp.plan_id = dtr.recommendedPlanId
    JOIN sys.query_store_query AS qsq
        ON qsq.query_id = rp.query_id
    JOIN sys.query_store_query_text AS qsqt
        ON qsqt.query_text_id = qsq.query_text_id;
```

These recommendations are just that, recommendations. While SQL Server is very good at making these based on the behavior captured through Query Store, until you enable Automatic Tuning, you can use these recommendations on your systems manually if you want. One thing you need to know about sys.dm_db_tuning_ recommendations is that the information is not persisted. In a failover, reboot, or other type of outage, this data will be reset. Any plans forced through Automatic Tuning will remain forced. However, you'll lose a history for why that plan was forced. You may want to capture this information regularly into other locations just in case.

Enabling Automatic Tuning

There are different ways to enable Automatic Tuning depending on if you're working within SQL Server 2019 or Azure SQL Database. If you're working with SQL Server 2017 or greater, you can use T-SQL to enable it. If you're working with Azure SQL Database, you can use T-SQL or the Azure portal. The T-SQL for both is the same, as is all the other queries you would run to look at the information. We'll start with Azure so you can see what that looks like.

Automatic Tuning in Azure SQL Database

Before we go on, please note that Azure is updated extremely frequently. The GUI that you see after you get this book could be different than that shown here. The processes should remain basically the same.

Connecting to a database within the portal and then scrolling to the bottom of the page, you should see something like Figure 8-5:

Figure 8-5. Automatic Tuning in the Azure portal, not currently configured

If you have not yet enabled Automatic Tuning, as you can see, it will show as "Not Configured" in the portal. You can click on this and it will open a new blade as shown in Figure 8-6:

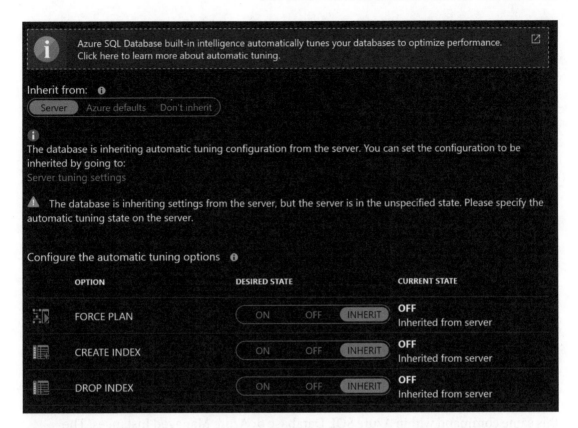

Figure 8-6. *Settings for Automatic Tuning on a database in the Azure portal*

Everything is explained fairly clearly on the blade. You can inherit from the server that contains the database, from the Azure defaults, or change the setting to not inheriting from anywhere. You can see a warning that while we're inheriting currently from the server, the server itself is not configured. We can make the change there, but for our purposes, we'll make the change right here. You can see at the bottom of the screen that in addition to forcing a plan, you can also have Azure SQL Database create or drop indexes. The index functionality is not directly related to Query Store, so we won't cover it here. To enable the forcing of the last known good plan, we just have to click ON as you can see in Figure 8-7:

Configure the automatic tuning options ⓘ		
OPTION	**DESIRED STATE**	**CURRENT STATE**
⚏ FORCE PLAN	(ON) OFF INHERIT	**OFF** Inherited from server
⚏ CREATE INDEX	ON OFF (INHERIT)	**OFF** Inherited from server
⚏ DROP INDEX	ON OFF (INHERIT)	**OFF** Inherited from server

***Figure 8-7.** Enabling Automatic Tuning in Azure SQL Database*

To complete this process, you will click the Apply button at the top of the page. It will prompt you to be sure that's the action you want. Once you click OK, Automatic Tuning is enabled on your database. No other actions are required.

Enable Automatic Tuning with T-SQL

There is no graphical interface for enabling automatic query tuning within Management Studio as I type this. Instead, you have to use a T-SQL command. You can also use this same command within Azure SQL Database or Azure Managed Instances. The command is as follows:

```
ALTER DATABASE current SET AUTOMATIC_TUNING (FORCE_LAST_GOOD_PLAN = ON);
```

You can of course substitute the appropriate database name for the default value of current that I use here. This command can only be run on one database at a time. If you wish to enable automatic tuning for all databases on your instance, you either have to enable it in the model database before those other databases are created, or you need to set it to on for each database on the server.

The only option currently for automatic_tuning is to do as we have done and enable the forcing of the last good plan. You can disable this by using the following command:

```
ALTER DATABASE current SET AUTOMATIC_TUNING (FORCE_LAST_GOOD_PLAN = OFF);
```

It's that easy. No other actions are necessary and this doesn't require a reboot or changes to the server itself.

Automatic Tuning at Work

In order to see Automatic Tuning at work, after we enable it and Query Store, we just have to rerun the script above. However, to ensure that the tests run successfully, we're going to clear Query Store and the cache so that everything is starting from scratch. This is the updated script:

```
ALTER DATABASE SCOPED CONFIGURATION CLEAR PROCEDURE_CACHE;
GO
ALTER DATABASE AdventureWorks SET QUERY_STORE CLEAR;
GO

EXEC dbo.ProductByCost @ActualCost = 8.2205;
GO 30

--remove the plan from cache
DECLARE @PlanHandle VARBINARY(64);
SELECT  @PlanHandle = deps.plan_handle
FROM    sys.dm_exec_procedure_stats AS deps
WHERE   deps.object_id = OBJECT_ID('dbo.ProductByCost');
IF @PlanHandle IS NOT NULL
    BEGIN
        DBCC FREEPROCCACHE(@PlanHandle);
    END
GO

--execute a query that will result in a different plan
EXEC dbo.ProductByCost @ActualCost = 0.0;
GO

--establish a new history of poor performance
EXEC dbo.ProductByCost @ActualCost = 8.2205;
GO 15
```

After executing this script, we'll want to go back and query sys.dm_db_tuning_recommendations. Figure 8-8 shows how the data there has now changed:

query_id	reason	score	CurrentState	CurrentStateReason
1	Average query CPU time changed from 0.15ms to 53...	36	Verifying	LastGoodPlanForced

Figure 8-8. *The regression has been fixed by Automatic Tuning*

The CurrentState value has been changed to Verifying. It will measure performance over a number of executions, much as it did before. If the performance degrades, it will unforce the plan. Further, if there are errors such as time outs or aborted executions, the plan will also be unforced. You'll also see the error_prone column in sys.dm_db_tuning_recommendations changed to a value of "Yes" in this event.

If you restart the server, the information in sys.dm_db_tuning_recommendations will be removed. Also, any plans that have been forced will also be removed. As soon as a query regresses again, any plan forcing will be automatically re-enabled. If this is an issue, you can always force the plan manually.

If a query is forced and then performance degrades, it will be unforced, as already noted. If that query again suffers from degraded performance, plan forcing will be removed and the query will be marked such that, at least until a server reboot when the information is removed, it will not be forced again.

Query Store Wait Statistics

The information we've talked about throughout the book that Query Store captures for query performance behavior changes the way lots of people do monitoring and query tuning. The addition of wait statistics for a given query adds to those changes. Now, you can get the wait statistics for a query easily. This information is aggregated using the time interval that you're aggregating your queries with, 60 minutes by default. Further, because there are so many waits, rather than list them all individually, the wait statistics in Query Store are grouped into categories of waits. If you need individual, detailed, wait statistics on a query, you'll need to use other mechanisms to capture the data.

Wait Statistics Categories

There's not much to say about the categories. You need to know how the categories are broken down in order to understand what waits they represent. Other than that, there's no additional functionality associated with them. This is purely informational so that you can correctly interpret the information when you look at the wait statistics in Query Store.

Table 8-2 shows the categories and the associated waits as published by Microsoft. Following their convention, percent signs (%) represent wild cards.

Table 8-2. *Query Store wait statistics categories and waits*

Integer value	Wait category	Wait types include in the category
0	Unknown	Unknown
1	CPU	SOS_SCHEDULER_YIELD
2	Worker thread	THREADPOOL
3	Lock	LCK_M_%
4	Latch	LATCH_%
5	Buffer latch	PAGELATCH_%
6	Buffer I/O	PAGEIOLATCH_%
7	Compilation*	RESOURCE_SEMAPHORE_QUERY_COMPILE
8	SQL CLR	CLR%, SQLCLR%
9	Mirroring	DBMIRROR%
10	Transaction	XACT%, DTC%, TRAN_MARKLATCH_%, MSQL_XACT_%, TRANSACTION_MUTEX
11	Idle	SLEEP_%, LAZYWRITER_SLEEP, SQLTRACE_BUFFER_FLUSH, SQLTRACE_INCREMENTAL_FLUSH_SLEEP, SQLTRACE_WAIT_ENTRIES, FT_IFTS_SCHEDULER_IDLE_WAIT, XE_DISPATCHER_WAIT, REQUEST_FOR_DEADLOCK_SEARCH, LOGMGR_QUEUE, ONDEMAND_TASK_QUEUE, CHECKPOINT_QUEUE, XE_TIMER_EVENT
12	Preemptive	PREEMPTIVE_%
13	Service broker	BROKER_% (but not BROKER_RECEIVE_WAITFOR)
14	Tran log I/O	LOGMGR, LOGBUFFER, LOGMGR_RESERVE_APPEND, LOGMGR_FLUSH, LOGMGR_PMM_LOG, CHKPT, WRITELOG
15	Network I/O	ASYNC_NETWORK_IO, NET_WAITFOR_PACKET, PROXY_NETWORK_IO, EXTERNAL_SCRIPT_NETWORK_IOF

(continued)

Table 8-2. (*continued*)

Integer value	Wait category	Wait types include in the category
16	Parallelism	CXPACKET, EXCHANGE
17	Memory	RESOURCE_SEMAPHORE, CMEMTHREAD, CMEMPARTITIONED, EE_PMOLOCK, MEMORY_ ALLOCATION_EXT, RESERVED_MEMORY_ALLOCATION_EXT, MEMORY_GRANT_UPDATE
18	User wait	WAITFOR, WAIT_FOR_RESULTS, BROKER_RECEIVE_ WAITFOR
19	Tracing	TRACEWRITE, SQLTRACE_LOCK, SQLTRACE_FILE_BUFFER, SQLTRACE_FILE_WRITE_IO_COMPLETION, SQLTRACE_ FILE_READ_IO_COMPLETION, SQLTRACE_PENDING_ BUFFER_WRITERS, SQLTRACE_SHUTDOWN, QUERY_ TRACEOUT, TRACE_EVTNOTIFF
20	Full text search	FT_RESTART_CRAWL, FULLTEXT GATHERER, MSSEARCH, FT_METADATA_MUTEX, FT_IFTSHC_MUTEX, FT_IFTSISM_ MUTEX, FT_IFTS_RWLOCK, FT_COMPROWSET_RWLOCK, FT_MASTER_MERGE, FT_PROPERTYLIST_CACHE, FT_MASTER_MERGE_COORDINATOR, PWAIT_RESOURCE_ SEMAPHORE_FT_PARALLEL_QUERY_SYNC
21	Other disk I/O	ASYNC_IO_COMPLETION, IO_COMPLETION, BACKUPIO, WRITE_COMPLETION, IO_QUEUE_LIMIT, IO_RETRY
22	Replication	SE_REPL_%, REPL_%, HADR_% (but not HADR_ THROTTLE_LOG_RATE_GOVERNOR), PWAIT_HADR_%, REPLICA_WRITES, FCB_REPLICA_WRITE, FCB_REPLICA_ READ, PWAIT_HADRSIM
23	Log rate governor	LOG_RATE_GOVERNOR, POOL_LOG_RATE_GOVERNOR, HADR_THROTTLE_LOG_RATE_GOVERNOR, INSTANCE_ LOG_RATE_GOVERNOR

Looking at Query Store Wait Statistics

There are two ways you can look at the wait statistics for a query within the Query Store. You can use T-SQL to query the information, or, there is a report within SQL Server Management Studio 18. We'll start by querying the wait statistics.

Querying Wait Statistics

Querying the wait statistics in Query Store is very straightforward. The most important thing to remember is that the statistics are aggregated through the time interval. While you can leave this off when you query the statistics, doing so then requires you to aggregate the aggregates in order to arrive at meaningful data. Here's an example query that looks at the wait statistics for the stored procedure we used earlier in the chapter:

```
SELECT qsws.wait_category_desc,
       qsws.total_query_wait_time_ms,
       qsws.avg_query_wait_time_ms,
       qsws.stdev_query_wait_time_ms
FROM sys.query_store_query AS qsq
    JOIN sys.query_store_plan AS qsp
        ON qsp.query_id = qsq.query_id
    JOIN sys.query_store_wait_stats AS qsws
        ON qsws.plan_id = qsp.plan_id
    JOIN sys.query_store_runtime_stats_interval AS qsrsi
        ON qsrsi.runtime_stats_interval_id = qsws.runtime_stats_interval_id
WHERE qsq.object_id = OBJECT_ID('dbo.ProductByCost');
```

You can see the results in Figure 8-9:

wait_category_desc	total_query_wait_time_ms	avg_query_wait_time_ms	stdev_query_wait_time_ms	start_time	end_time
CPU	10097	631.0625	1747.54082069633	2019-05-11 15:00:00.0000000 +00:00	2019-05-11 16:00:00.0000000 +00:00
Network IO	954	59.625	231.140931035591	2019-05-11 15:00:00.0000000 +00:00	2019-05-11 16:00:00.0000000 +00:00
CPU	4667	311.133333333333	184.384923461762	2019-05-11 17:00:00.0000000 +00:00	2019-05-11 18:00:00.0000000 +00:00

Figure 8-9. *Wait statistics for dbo.ProductbyCost*

You can see that there are two different time intervals with different wait statistics. The only waits experienced by the query were in the CPU and Network I/O categories. Using the table from the section above, that means that the waits experienced could be any of these in Table 8-3:

Table 8-3.   *The waits experienced by dbo.ProductByCost*

Network IO	ASYNC_NETWORK_IO, NET_WAITFOR_PACKET, PROXY_NETWORK_IO, EXTERNAL_SCRIPT_NETWORK_IOF
CPU	SOS_SCHEDULER_YIELD

Clearly, this makes for a quick and easy way to understand the bottleneck experience by a query. However, that will be a general set of knowledge, not detailed. Still, it makes a huge difference in our ability to easily identify problems that need our attention.

Wait Statistics Report

Chapter 4 is going to cover the Query Store reports in detail. Here I'll just show the general behavior of the report itself. Upon opening the report, you'll see something similar to Figure 8-10:

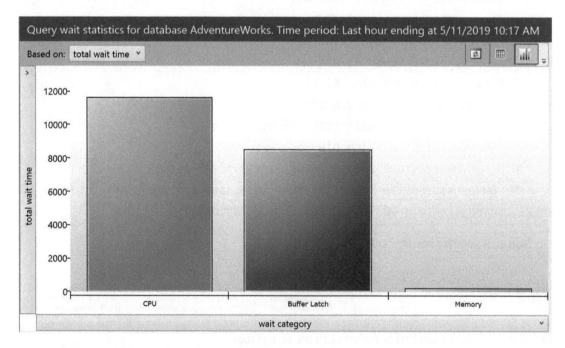

Figure 8-10.   *Wait statistics report showing aggregate information*

When you first open the report, only aggregate information for the time period is shown. You're seeing all the queries and the various waits with a given category. If you then click on a category, such as the CPU wait that you see, the view will change to something like Figure 8-11:

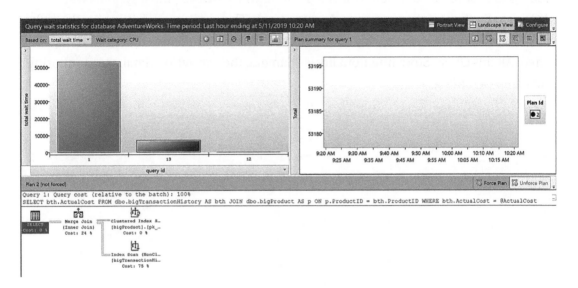

Figure 8-11. *Report showing all queries that have experienced the wait selected*

What is now shown in the report is a series of queries in the upper left that have experienced the wait that was selected. Then, the report functions much as other reports do. Selecting a query shows its various query plans over time on the right. Selecting any of those plans will cause the full plan to be shown in the pane at the bottom of the screen. In our instance you can see that the query with the most waits was dbo. ProductByCost. Specifically, it was the bad plan from our original example at the start of the chapter.

All this provides a way to understand not simply query performance, but the waits affecting the query as well.

Conclusion

Query Store enables a bunch of interesting scenarios and Automatic Tuning to eliminate plan regression is one of the more exciting. As with all else, you should monitor your systems to ensure that this behavior is benefiting you. However, most systems will likely benefit, thus freeing you up to do other work. That work may entail using the wait statistics that are now stored with queries to better identify the ones that need to be tuned. All this Query Store functionality is changing the way we do database monitoring and database tuning.

CHAPTER 9

Troubleshooting Issues with Query Store

Like any other aspect of SQL Server, most of the time, you can simply turn Query Store on and then not worry about it. However, like any other aspect of SQL Server, things can go wrong. There are two tools that you can use to understand what is happening with Query Store on your database:

- Query Store specific wait statistics

- Extended Events for Query Store

This chapter will look at some common problems that can arise with Query Store and how you can use the tools provided in order to ensure that Query Store is working well on your systems.

Query Store Waits

By design, as we described in the first couple of chapters, Query Store is designed to be as unobtrusive as possible. In physics, the observer effect says that observation of a process or object can affect the behavior of that process or object. Similarly in SQL Server, however lightweight the data collection, the act of collecting information is adding some additional load to your SQL Server instance. The number of possible factors that can lead to issues with the Query Store is huge. It is the same list as any other process within SQL Server: the amount of memory and CPU you have available; the number, size, and volume of the transactions in your system; the number and speed of your disks and disk controllers, and, frankly, the code running in your T-SQL statements. Any or all of these and more can change the behavior of Query Store.

© Tracy Boggiano and Grant Fritchey 2019

T. Boggiano and G. Fritchey, *Query Store for SQL Server 2019*, https://doi.org/10.1007/978-1-4842-5004-4_9

The first way we can understand Query Store behavior is to use the wait statistics. Generally speaking, wait statistics are always the best way to gain a general understanding of the behavior of any given system. If you know what the system is waiting on, you know where your bottlenecks are. There are two ways to look at waits in the Query Store, through the traditional dynamic management view, sy.dm_os_wait_stats, or, on Azure SQL Database, sys.dm_db_wait_stats. You can also use Extended Events wait_completed to see waits, but that's a very granular approach and won't generally be needed. We'll focus only on the DMV.

When talking about querying the wait statistics within SQL Server, I recommend you start with Paul Randal's scripts. The import of these scripts is that they eliminate the noise, the wait statistics that never mean anything. You can access those scripts here: `https://bit.ly/2wsQHQE`.

Query Store wait statistics have a common naming convention. They always start with "qds_". To see just the wait statistics coming from Query Store, you would run this query in Listing 9-1:

Listing 9-1. Wait Statistics coming from Query Store

```
SELECT dows.wait_type,
       dows.waiting_tasks_count,
       dows.wait_time_ms,
       dows.max_wait_time_ms,
       dows.signal_wait_time_ms
FROM sys.dm_os_wait_stats AS dows
WHERE dows.wait_type LIKE 'qds_%';
```

The results would look something like Figure 9-1:

	wait_type	waiting_tasks_count	wait_time_ms	max_wait_time_ms	signal_wait_time_ms
1	QDS_DYN_VECTOR	0	0	0	0
2	QDS_STMT	0	0	0	0
3	QDS_CTXS	0	0	0	0
4	QDS_BCKG_TASK	0	0	0	0
5	QDS_DB_DISK	0	0	0	0
6	QDS_STMT_DISK	0	0	0	0
7	QDS_ASYNC_PERSIST_TASK	0	0	0	0
8	QDS_LOADDB	0	0	0	0
9	QDS_ASYNC_PERSIST_TASK_START	1	170	170	0
10	QDS_ASYNC_CHECK_CONSISTENCY_TASK	0	0	0	0
11	QDS_TASK_START	1	24	24	4
12	QDS_PERSIST_TASK_MAIN_LOOP_SLEEP	1105	132103279	21616262	243034
13	QDS_TASK_SHUTDOWN	0	0	0	0
14	QDS_SHUTDOWN_QUEUE	0	0	0	0
15	QDS_EXCLUSIVE_ACCESS	0	0	0	0
16	QDS_CLEANUP_STALE_QUERIES_TASK_MAIN_LOOP_SLEEP	0	0	0	0
17	QDS_ASYNC_QUEUE	1	0	0	0
18	QDS_BLOOM_FILTER	0	0	0	0
19	QDS_QDS_CAPTURE_INIT	0	0	0	0
20	QDS_HOST_INIT	0	0	0	0

Figure 9-1. *All the Query Store wait statistics*

Of course, your system will have different values in each of the columns, but you should see a similar list of waits. You would not normally look at the Query Store wait statistics in isolation. Instead, you would query the wait statistics and look for the top ones on your system. When those top waits are Query Store, you're likely experiencing some sort of issue.

However, there are just a few Query Store waits that you can safely ignore. Paul Randal also maintains a library of wait statistics (accessible here: `https://bit.ly/2ePzYO2`). Based on his documentation, there are three waits, currently, that you can safely ignore when it comes to Query Store:

```
qds_async_queue
qds_cleanup_stale_queries_task_main_loop_sleep
qds_shutdown_queue
```

You would not simply query for the Query Store waits. Instead, as part of your normal monitoring of wait statistics on your system, you would look for the waits above because they would indicate Query Store itself, its operations, is leading to issues on your system. If you see any of the "qds_*" waits in your top 10, you would want to understand what that wait statistics is and then drill down on why it's causing problems for you in your system. The way we drill down when monitoring Query Store is to use Extended Events.

Extended Events and Query Store

Extended Events are the best method to do a detailed analysis of the behavior of Query Store in your systems. Extended Events are a fairly dense topic that we're not going to try to explain in detail in this book. To get started with Extended Events, I suggest first the Microsoft documentation here: `https://bit.ly/2LfWMoj`. Once you're comfortable with how Extended Events works, you can more easily explore the capabilities of monitoring Query Store using Extended Events.

At this writing, there are currently 92 events within the qds, Query Data Store, package defined within SQL Server 2019. You can easily list them if you want to run a query as follows in Listing 9-2:

Listing 9-2. List Query Data Store Extended Events

```
SELECT dxo.name,
       dxo.description
FROM sys.dm_xe_packages AS dxp
    JOIN sys.dm_xe_objects AS dxo
        ON dxp.guid = dxo.package_guid
WHERE dxp.name = 'qds'
AND dxo.object_type = 'event';
```

Another way to access the information is through the Extended Events GUI within SQL Server Management Studio as shown in Figure 9-2:

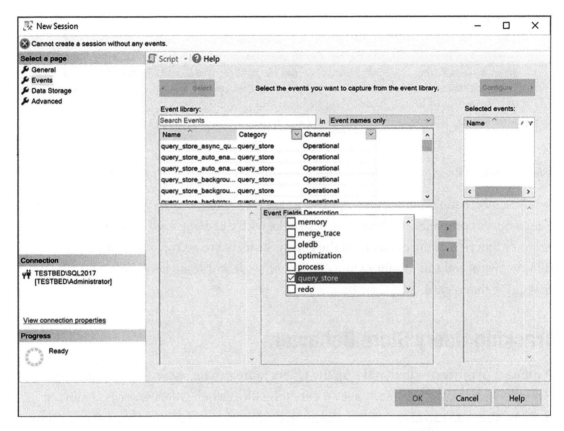

Figure 9-2. *Selecting only the Query Store events in Extended Events*

The only issue here is that not all these events are active. Many of them, maybe even most of them, are only accessible through special flags set by Microsoft. So, while you can see them, even add them to a session, no activity will ever be recorded by them.

As is normal with every other event in Extended Events, the Query Store events will have a name, a description, and a defined set of columns associated with the event. So, if we were to monitor the behavior of Query Store using Extended Events, one event we might be interested in is the query_store_size_retention_cleanup_finished event. Selecting that event, we can then see the information that Query Store itself is gathering as you can see in Figure 9-3:

Event Fields	Description
database_id	ID of the database for which Query Store size based retention policy cle...
deleted_plan_count	The number of query plans that has been deleted from the Query Store ...
deleted_query_count	The number of queries that has been deleted from the Query Store as p...
estimated_deleted_size_kb	Estimated amount of data that the clean-up task has managed to delete ...
last_deleted_query_total_c...	Total CPU of the last evicted query.
max_deleted_total_cpu	Max total CPU of all deleted queries
query_cost	Cost of the last evicted query.

Figure 9-3. *The information captured by query_store_execution_runtime_info*

The information in this event represents the data that the Query Store is capturing after a query completes its cleanup process. So, with this event, you could observe and monitor that part of the behavior of the Query Store. We're going to look at a couple of different ways you can monitor Query Store behavior and some very particular events that aid in that regard.

Tracking Query Store Behaviors

A number of processes that make up the Query Store can be observed by capturing Extended Events. We've already see an event that fires when Query Store is cleansing itself for size. You can also watch a matching event, query_store_size_retention_cleanup_started to see when this event begins. For general observation of Query Store behavior, Listing 9-3 contains a set of events that, as of this writing, I know will fire to produce information about the standard behavior of Query Store:

Listing 9-3. Extended Event Session producing information on the standard behavior of Query Store

```
CREATE EVENT SESSION QueryStoreBehavior
ON SERVER
    ADD EVENT qds.query_store_background_task_persist_finished,
    ADD EVENT qds.query_store_background_task_persist_started,
    ADD EVENT qds.query_store_capture_policy_evaluate,
    ADD EVENT qds.query_store_capture_policy_start_capture,
    ADD EVENT qds.query_store_database_out_of_disk_space,
    ADD EVENT qds.query_store_db_cleared,
    ADD EVENT qds.query_store_db_diagnostics,
    ADD EVENT qds.query_store_db_settings_changed,
```

```
    ADD EVENT qds.query_store_plan_removal,
    ADD EVENT qds.query_store_size_retention_cleanup_finished,
    ADD EVENT qds.query_store_size_retention_cleanup_started
    ADD TARGET package0.event_file
    (SET filename = N'C:\ExEvents\QueryStorePlanForcing.xel', max_rollover_
    files = (3))
WITH (TRACK_CAUSALITY = ON);
```

These events capture some of the behaviors of the Query Store. If you create this session, start it, and watch the Live Data window in SSMS, we can actually see some of the events fire if we manipulate queries and the Query Store itself. Let's fire a few commands to see this in action. To start with, we'll clear the Query Store with the code in Listing 9-4:

Listing 9-4. Clear Query Store

```
ALTER DATABASE AdventureWorks SET QUERY_STORE CLEAR;
```

This will fire the event, query_store_db_cleared, as we see in Figure 9-4:

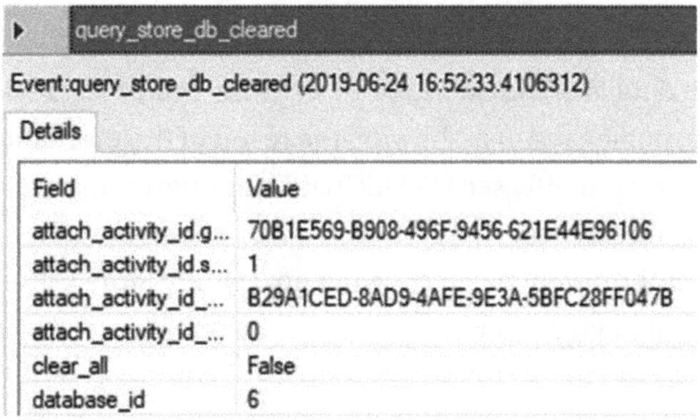

Figure 9-4. *query_store_db_cleared event captured for a given database*

The first four columns are for managing the Extended Events causality tracking, showing the distinct grouping of events and the order in which they occur. We can ignore that in this instance. What we see are the clear_all setting, which is defined in the QUERY_STORE CLEAR command, which can be set to clear ALL.

To see the next event, we'll run the following stored procedure in Listing 9-5 from the previous chapter:

Listing 9-5. Call stored procedure

```
EXEC dbo.AddressByCity @City = N'London';
```

We'll get the following two events, related and in the order in which they are firing as shown in Figure 9-5:

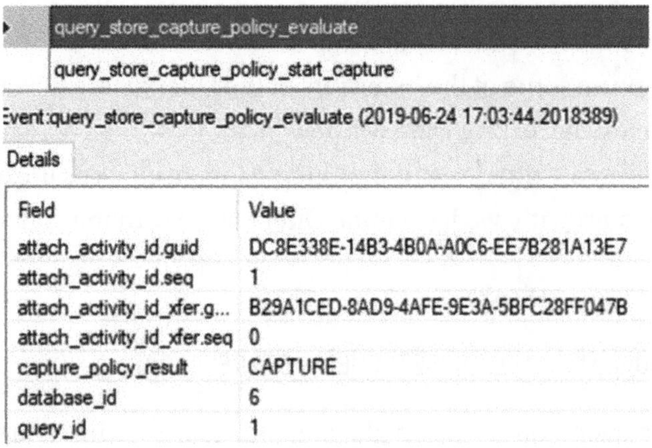

Figure 9-5. *Query Store evaluates a query and then captures it*

I'm showing the details of the query_store_capture_policy_evaluate event. You can see that the capture_policy_result is showing the result of the evaluation, in this case, CAPTURE. You'll also frequently see UNDECIDED for queries that have been evaluated but are not going to be captured.

You may see an intermittent event showing how Query Store self-evaluates on a regular basis as shown in Figure 9-6:

Field	Value
▶ query_store_db_diagnostics	

Event:query_store_db_diagnostics (2019-06-24 17:08:32.1083664)

Details

Field	Value
attach_activity_id.guid	F0DC67B6-0B96-49B6-8755-4E56AD1C8EA4
attach_activity_id.seq	3
capture_policy_mode	x_qdsCaptureModeAll
context_settings_memor...	0
current_buffered_items_...	16
current_stmt_hash_map...	104
database_id	6
db_state_actual	2
db_state_desired	2
flush_interval_seconds	120
interval_length_minutes	60
max_buffered_items_size...	6187816
max_memory_available_kb	6187816
max_plans_per_query	200
max_size_mb	1000
max_stmt_hash_map_siz...	6187816
pending_persistance_me...	16
plan_count	1
plans_used_last_day	1
plans_used_last_hour	1
queries_used_last_day	1
queries_used_last_hour	1
query_count	1
query_store_read_only_r...	0
query_text_count	1
runtime_stats_memory_u...	1
size_based_cleanup_mo...	x_qdsSizeBasedCleanupModeAuto
size_based_cleanup_per...	80
size_based_cleanup_per...	90
stale_query_threshold_d...	30
undecided_queries_wind...	0
undecided_query_count	0
wait_stats_capture_mode	x_qdsWaitStatsCaptureModeMax

Figure 9-6. *Settings and diagnostics of Query Store*

You can see the current settings for Query Store, such as the plans per query limit, currently set at 200. You also get to see the plans and plan use being managed by Query Store. These numbers will obviously change over time, showing the behavior of Query Store over time.

Let's take a look at one more of the events in action. Run the following code in Listing 9-6 to remove a plan from the plan cache:

Listing 9-6. Remove a plan from cache

```
DECLARE @PlanID INT;

SELECT TOP 1
        @PlanID = qsp.plan_id
FROM    sys.query_store_query AS qsq
JOIN    sys.query_store_plan AS qsp
        ON qsp.query_id = qsq.query_id
WHERE   qsq.object_id = OBJECT_ID('dbo.AddressByCity');

EXEC sys.sp_query_store_remove_plan @plan_id = @PlanID;
```

We can then see this event as shown in Figure 9-7:

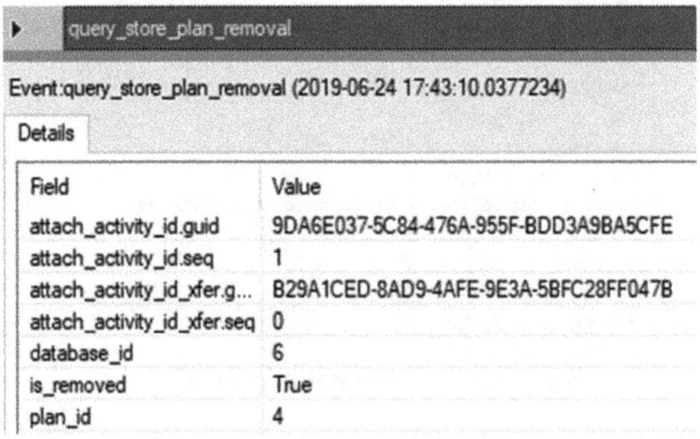
query_store_plan_removal
Event:query_store_plan_removal (2019-06-24 17:43:10.0377234)
Details
Field
Value
attach_activity_id.guid
9DA6E037-5C84-476A-955F-BDD3A9BA5CFE
attach_activity_id.seq
1
attach_activity_id_xfer.g...
B29A1CED-8AD9-4AFE-9E3A-5BFC28FF047B
attach_activity_id_xfer.seq
0
database_id
6
is_removed
True
plan_id
4

Figure 9-7. *Plan removed from Query Store*

You can see the database, the fact that plan was successfully removed, and the plan being removed.

All these events give you a good idea of what's happening within Query Store, allowing you to see how Query Store behaves.

Conclusion

While you really should just see normal behavior from Query Store the vast majority of the time, it is possible for things to go wrong. Knowing how to monitor Query Store itself ensures that you have a higher degree of confidence that Query Store is supporting and helping you, not hurting you. Wait statistics are going to be the principal mechanism of assuring good Query Store behavior. You can drill down on the details of that behavior using Extended Events to see exactly how the system is working. These processes should enable you to protect your systems and better understand the behavior of Query Store.

CHAPTER 10

Community Tools

A few community tools have been developed to help with configuration and harvesting of the data in Query Store. dbatools is a community-driven PowerShell module that includes three cmdlets for helping you configure Query Store. The First Responder Kit contains a set of stored procedures including one that queries Query Store data. In this chapter we will cover these tools to how they can help see the options of Query Store, set the options of Query Store, and harvest the data in Query Store.

dbatools

dbatools is a PowerShell open source module developed with currently over 400 commands to help manage SQL Server. There currently are three commands for Query Store: `Get-DbaDbQueryStoreOption`, `Set-DbaDbQueryStoreOption,` and `Copy-DbaQueryStoreConfig`. By using dbatools, you can retrieve and set the settings across multiple databases and servers at the same time. Full documentation and information on dbatools can be found at `http://dbatools.io` and installed on any machine with PowerShell 5 or higher by running the code in Listing 10-1 at a PowerShell command prompt.

Listing 10-1. Install dbatools

```
Install-Module dbatools
```

Get-DbaDbQueryStoreOption

The first command from dbatools we will explore is `Get-DbaDbQueryStoreOption`. This command retrieves the Query Store options that have been set on a database. There are several ways to run the command to return the data. Listing 10-2 will return the Query Store options for all databases on the server specified except master and tempdb

© Tracy Boggiano and Grant Fritchey 2019
T. Boggiano and G. Fritchey, *Query Store for SQL Server 2019*, https://doi.org/10.1007/978-1-4842-5004-4_10

because you cannot use Query Store with those databases. The results of the code from Listing 10-2 can be seen in Figure 10-1.

Listing 10-2. Return all the Query Store options for all the databases on the specified server

```
Get-DbaDbQueryStoreOption -SqlInstance MyServer
```

```
ComputerName                            : WIN-IORMK3CO8VS
InstanceName                            : MSSQLSERVER
SqlInstance                             : WIN-IORMK3CO8VS
Database                                : msdb
ActualState                             : Off
DataFlushIntervalInSeconds              : 900
StatisticsCollectionIntervalInMinutes   : 60
MaxStorageSizeInMB                      : 1000
CurrentStorageSizeInMB                  : 0
QueryCaptureMode                        : Auto
SizeBasedCleanupMode                    : Auto
StaleQueryThresholdInDays               : 30

ComputerName                            : WIN-IORMK3CO8VS
InstanceName                            : MSSQLSERVER
SqlInstance                             : WIN-IORMK3CO8VS
Database                                : AdventureWorks
ActualState                             : ReadWrite
DataFlushIntervalInSeconds              : 900
StatisticsCollectionIntervalInMinutes   : 60
MaxStorageSizeInMB                      : 1024
CurrentStorageSizeInMB                  : 0
QueryCaptureMode                        : 4
SizeBasedCleanupMode                    : Auto
StaleQueryThresholdInDays               : 90
```

Figure 10-1. *The output from Get-DbaDbQueryStoreOption for the whole SQL Server instance*

To see the settings for a particular database, you can run the code in Listing 10-3. The results are show in Figure 10-2.

Listing 10-3. Return all the Query Store options for the AdventureWorks database

```
Get-DbaDbQueryStoreOption -SqlInstance MyServer
    -Database AdventureWorks
```

```
ComputerName                           : WIN-IORMK3C08VS
InstanceName                           : MSSQLSERVER
SqlInstance                            : WIN-IORMK3C08VS
Database                               : AdventureWorks
ActualState                            : ReadWrite
DataFlushIntervalInSeconds             : 900
StatisticsCollectionIntervalInMinutes  : 60
MaxStorageSizeInMB                     : 1024
CurrentStorageSizeInMB                 : 0
QueryCaptureMode                       : 4
SizeBasedCleanupMode                   : Auto
StaleQueryThresholdInDays              : 90
```

Figure 10-2. *The output from Get-DbaDbQueryStoreOption for the AdventureWorks database*

The results if you have several databases on one server can be hard to read and require a lot of scrolling, but there is an option to get this data back in a table format. See the code in Listing 10-4 for how to accomplish this. Part of the results from the code in Listing 10-4 can be seen in Figure 10-3.

Listing 10-4. Return Query Store settings in table format

```
Get-DbaDbQueryStoreOption -SqlInstance MyServer | Format-Table
    -AutoSize -Wrap
```

```
ComputerName    InstanceName SqlInstance     Database       ActualState DataFlushIntervalInSeconds
------------    ------------ -----------     --------       ----------- --------------------------
WIN-IORMK3C08VS MSSQLSERVER  WIN-IORMK3C08VS AdventureWorks ReadWrite                          900
```

Figure 10-3. *The output from Get-DbaDbQueryStoreOption in table format*

Lastly, you can use the Get-DbaDbQueryStoreOption command to return all the databases with a particular configuration setting. In the following example, we will return all the databases that have the ActualState of Query Store as ReadWrite as seen in Listing 10-5. The results of the code in Listing 10-5 can be seen in Figure 10-4.

Listing 10-5. Return database where Query Store ActualState is ReadWrite

```
Get-DbaDbQueryStoreOption -SqlInstance MyServer | Where-Object
    {$_.ActualState -eq "ReadWrite"}
```

```
ComputerName                            : WIN-IORMK3C08VS
InstanceName                            : MSSQLSERVER
SqlInstance                             : WIN-IORMK3C08VS
Database                                : AdventureWorks
ActualState                             : ReadWrite
DataFlushIntervalInSeconds              : 900
StatisticsCollectionIntervalInMinutes   : 60
MaxStorageSizeInMB                      : 1024
CurrentStorageSizeInMB                  : 0
QueryCaptureMode                        : 4
SizeBasedCleanupMode                    : Auto
StaleQueryThresholdInDays               : 90
```

Figure 10-4. *The output from Get-DbaDbQueryStoreOption for ReadWrite Query Store databases*

More parameters can be found for this command online at the dbatools website (https://dbatools.io).

Set-DbaDbQueryStoreOption

The second command from dbatools we will explore is Set-DbaDbQueryStoreOptions. This command sets the Query Store options that exists in the databases you specify. You can use the command to set just one setting or them all depending on your needs. We will, in Listing 10-6, set the Query Store options for the best practices laid out in Chapter 3 for all the databases on the SQL Server instance. The only exceptions to this configuration, if you remember from Chapter 3, would be if you needed a larger Query Store or if you wanted a different collection interval.

Listing 10-6. Use Set-DbaDbQueryStoreOption to set options on all the databases to best practices

```
Set-DbaDbQueryStoreOption -SqlInstance MyServer -State ReadWrite
    -FlushInterval 900 -CollectionInterval 60 -MaxSize 2048
    -CaptureMode AUTO -CleanupMode Auto -StaleQueryThreshold 30
```

After issuing the command from Listing 10-6, the command outputs the new settings for each database as you have seen before from the Get-DbaDbQueryStoreOption command. These can be seen in Figure 10-5.

```
ComputerName                            : WIN-IORMK3C08VS
InstanceName                            : MSSQLSERVER
SqlInstance                             : WIN-IORMK3C08VS
Database                                : msdb
ActualState                             : ReadWrite
DataFlushIntervalInSeconds              : 900
StatisticsCollectionIntervalInMinutes   : 60
MaxStorageSizeInMB                      : 2048
CurrentStorageSizeInMB                  : 0
QueryCaptureMode                        : Auto
SizeBasedCleanupMode                    : Auto
StaleQueryThresholdInDays               : 30

ComputerName                            : WIN-IORMK3C08VS
InstanceName                            : MSSQLSERVER
SqlInstance                             : WIN-IORMK3C08VS
Database                                : AdventureWorks
ActualState                             : ReadWrite
DataFlushIntervalInSeconds              : 900
StatisticsCollectionIntervalInMinutes   : 60
MaxStorageSizeInMB                      : 2048
CurrentStorageSizeInMB                  : 0
QueryCaptureMode                        : Auto
SizeBasedCleanupMode                    : Auto
StaleQueryThresholdInDays               : 30
```

Figure 10-5. *Output from Set-DbaDbQueryStoreOption for best practices*

It is possible, for example, to change the size of the particular database and the statistics collection interval if you need to, by using the code in Listing 10-6. This code allows you to keep more data at a more granular level. The output from the code in Listing 10-7 can be seen in Figure 10-6.

Listing 10-7. Use Set-DbaDbQueryStoreOption to change the size and collection interval for AdventureWorks

```
Set-DbaDbQueryStoreOption -SqlInstance MyServer
    -Database AdventureWorks -MaxSize 4096
    -CollectionInterval 15
```

```
ComputerName                             : WIN-IORMK3CO8VS
InstanceName                             : MSSQLSERVER
SqlInstance                              : WIN-IORMK3CO8VS
Database                                 : AdventureWorks
ActualState                              : ReadWrite
DataFlushIntervalInSeconds               : 900
StatisticsCollectionIntervalInMinutes    : 15
MaxStorageSizeInMB                       : 4096
CurrentStorageSizeInMB                   : 0
QueryCaptureMode                         : Auto
SizeBasedCleanupMode                     : Auto
StaleQueryThresholdInDays                : 30
```

Figure 10-6. *Output from Set-DbaDbQueryStoreOption changing max size and collection interval*

More parameters can be found for this command online at the dbatools website (`https://dbatools.io`).

Copy-DbaQueryStoreConfig

The last command we will explore is `Copy-DbaQueryStoreConfig`. This command can copy the Query Store options between databases on the same server or the settings from one database on one server to databases on another server, with the parameter `-AllDatabases`. Listing 10-8 will copy the options from MyServerA and the AdventureWorks database to all the databases on MyServerB.

Listing 10-8. Copy Query Store options from one database to all the databases on another server

```
Copy-DbaDbQueryStoreOption -Source MyServerA
    -SourceDatabase AdventureWorks -Destination MyServerB
    -AllDatabases
```

You may also copy the options to one database server on the destination database server using the code in Listing 10-9.

Listing 10-9. Copy Query Store options from one database to another database on another server

```
Copy-DbaDbQueryStoreOption -Source MyServerA
    -SourceDatabase AdventureWorks -Destination MyServerB
    -DestinationDatabase AdventuresWorksDW
```

dbatools Summary

In summary, we covered the three cmdlets in dbatools that help you see the configuration of Query Store and configure Query Store. The Get-DbaDbQueryStoreOption cmdlet allows you to view the options set for Query Store. The Set-DbaDbQueryStoreOptions cmdlet allows you to set the options for Query Store. The Copy-DbaQueryStoreConfig cmdlet allows you to copy configurations between databases and servers.

sp_BlitzQueryStore

sp_BlitzQueryStore is part of the First Responder Kit made by Brent Ozar, ULTD., located at http://FirstResponderKit.org. The whole kit can be downloaded from there, or you can install it using the code in Listing 10-10 if you have dbatools installed.

Listing 10-10. PowerShell to install First Responder Kit

```
Install-DbaFirstResponderKit -Server MyServer -Database master
```

The procedure by default looks at the data in Query Store for the last 7 days (by default), finds the times that consumed the most resources for each metric, and finds the top three queries (by default) that consumed the most resources for each metric. By analyzing by each time period and each metric, you can get a more balanced and targeted analysis of data from Query Store. For example, it will find the time period in the last 7 days where you did the most logical reads and return the top three queries doing the reads during that time period. Then you can dive in and try to figure out how to improve the performance for those queries during that time period

By default, you can execute the procedure with just the database you want to see data for, and it will return the top query for each metric for the last 7 days. Listing 10-11 shows you the T-SQL to execute to see the results. Figures 10-7 and 10-8 show some of the columns that are returned when you run the stored procedure.

Listing 10-11. Execute sp_BlitzQueryStore for the top query for each metric the last 7 days

```
EXEC sp_BlitzQueryStore @DatabaseName = 'AdventureWorks'
```

	database_name	query_cost	plan_id	query_id	query_id_all_plan_ids	query_sql_text	proc_or_function_name	query_plan_xml
1	AdventureWorks	48.15	46	213	46, 76	(@i int)SELECT ...	[dbo].[p_sel_get_sales_...	<ShowPlanXML x...
2	AdventureWorks	51.32	76	213	46, 76	(@i int)SELECT ...	[dbo].[p_sel_get_sales_...	<ShowPlanXML x...
3	AdventureWorks	7.55	49	216	49	SELECT p.Nam...	[dbo].[p_sel_discount_s...	<ShowPlanXML x...
4	AdventureWorks	7.55	53	223	53	SELECT p.Nam...	[dbo].[p_sel_prod_tble_...	<ShowPlanXML x...
5	AdventureWorks	7.54	50	217	50	SELECT 'Total i...	[dbo].[p_calc_revenue_...	<ShowPlanXML x...

Figure 10-7. *sp_BlitzQueryStore result set*

	warnings	pattern	parameter_sniffing_symptoms
1	Parallel, Multiple Plans, High tempdb use	avg cpu, avg duration, avg log bytes, avg logic...	Low physical reads sometimes
2	Parallel, Multiple Plans, High tempdb use	avg cpu, avg duration, avg log bytes, avg logic...	Too few executions to compare (< 2).
3	Parallel, Expensive Sort, Long Running With Low...	avg rows, max duration	Low physical reads sometimes, Low physical rea...
4	Parallel, Expensive Sort	avg rows	
5	Parallel, Expensive Sort	avg rows	High physical reads sometimes

Figure 10-8. *sp_BlitzQueryStore result set*

You can click on the `query_plan_xml` column and bring up the query plan to view and troubleshoot. Some analysis has been done for you by giving you the `top_three_ waits`, `missing_indexes`, and `implicit_conversion_info`. Other columns that returned are as follows:

- top_three_waits – with total ms in parentheses

- missing_indexes – listed from the missing index hints in the query plans

- implicit_conversion_info – listed from the query plan

- cached_execution_parameters

- count_executions

- count_compiles

- total_cpu_time

- avg_cpu_time

- total_duration

- avg_duration

- total_logical_io_reads

- avg_logical_io_reads

- total_physical_io_reads

- avg_physical_io_reads

- total_logical_io_writes

- avg_logical_io_writes

- total_rowcount

- avg_rowcount

- total_query_max_used_memory

- avg_query_max_used_memory

- total_tempdb_space_used

- avg_tempdb_space_used

- total_log_bytes_used

- avg_log_bytes_used

- total_num_physical_io_reads

- avg_num_physical_io_reads

- first_execution_time

- last_execution_time

- last_force_failure_reason_desc

- context_settings

You can see below the results returned that there is a detailed analysis of queries that were executed during that time period including if it finds problems with your execution plans, high tempdb usage, long-running queries but low CPU, and then it wraps up by identifying the worst times by each metric that the system was performing in. See Figure 10-9 for example of this output. This gives you the ability to drill down on specific poorly performing times or queries that are troublesome within the specified time period.

Note   Use the @TOP parameter to return more than the top one query. But use it cautiously as this procedure does a lot processing through the query plans. Recommendations are to limit to 10.

	Priority	FindingsGroup	Finding	URL	Details
1	100	Execution Plans	Expensive Sort	http://www.brentozar.com/blitzcache/expensive-s...	There's a sort in your plan that costs >=50% of t...
2	100	High tempdb use	This query uses more than half of a data file on ...	No URL yet	You should take a look at tempdb waits to see if ...
3	150	Long Running Low CPU	You have a query that runs for much longer than...	https://www.brentozar.com/blitzcache/long-runnin...	This can be a sign of blocking, linked servers, o...
4	200	Execution Plans	Multiple execution plans	http://brentozar.com/blitzcache/multiple-plans/	Queries exist with multiple execution plans (as d...
5	200	Execution Plans	Parallelism	http://brentozar.com/blitzcache/parallel-plans-dete...	Parallel plans detected. These warrant investiga...
6	255	Need more help?	Paste your plan on the internet!	http://pastetheplan.com	This makes it easy to share plans and post them...
7	255	Thanks for using sp_B...	From Your Community Volunteers	http://FirstResponderKit.org	We hope you found this tool useful. Current ver...
8	255	Worsts	Worst Avg CPU	N/A	Your worst avg cpu range was on 2019-03-04 b...
9	255	Worsts	Worst Avg Duration	N/A	Your worst avg duration range was on 2019-03-...
10	255	Worsts	Worst Avg Log Bytes	N/A	Your worst avg log bytes range was on 2019-03...
11	255	Worsts	Worst Avg Logical Reads	N/A	Your worst avg logical read range was on 2019-...
12	255	Worsts	Worst Avg Logical Writes	N/A	Your worst avg logical write range was on 2019-...
13	255	Worsts	Worst Avg Memory	N/A	Your worst avg memory range was on 2019-03-...
14	255	Worsts	Worst Avg Physical Reads	N/A	Your worst avg physical read range was on 201...
15	255	Worsts	Worst Avg tempdb	N/A	Your worst avg tempdb range was on 2019-03-...
16	255	Worsts	Worst Max CPU	N/A	Your worst max cpu range was on 2019-03-04 b...
17	255	Worsts	Worst Max Duration	N/A	Your worst max duration range was on 2019-03-...
18	255	Worsts	Worst Max Log Bytes	N/A	Your worst max log bytes range was on 2019-03...
19	255	Worsts	Worst Max Logical Reads	N/A	Your worst max logical read range was on 2019-...
20	255	Worsts	Worst Max Logical Writes	N/A	Your worst max logical write range was on 2019...
21	255	Worsts	Worst Max Memory	N/A	Your worst max memory range was on 2019-03-...
22	255	Worsts	Worst Max Physical Reads	N/A	Your worst max physical read range was on 201...
23	255	Worsts	Worst Max tempdb	N/A	Your worst max tempdb range was on 2019-03-...
24	255	Worsts	Worst Row Counts	N/A	Your worst avg row count range was on 2019-0...

Figure 10-9. *sp_BlitzQueryStore time period analysis*

There are other options for running this procedure; we will go through a few important ones to help you to get the data you need. In Listing 10-12 you can specify the date range you want to return in your output by specifying the @StateDate and @EndDate parameters.

Listing 10-12. Specify date range for sp_BlitzQueryStore

```
EXEC sp_BlitzQueryStore @DatabaseName = 'AdventureWorks',
    @StartDate = '20170526', @EndDate = '20170527'
```

If you are trying to troubleshoot a specific stored procedure, you can look for that stored procedure specifically. In Listing 10-13 you will find the code on how to return the top statement in the procedure MyStoredProcedure by specifying the @StoredProcName parameter.

Listing 10-13. Return top statement for a specific stored procedure

```
EXEC sp_BlitzQueryStore @DatabaseName = 'AdventureWorks',
    @Top = 1, @StoredProcName = 'MyStoredProcedure'
```

You can also use it to look at failed queries by specifying the @Failed parameter. Listing 10-14 is an example of how to return the top query that has failed.

Listing 10-14. Return top failed query

```
EXEC sp_BlitzQueryStore @DatabaseName = 'AdventureWorks',
    @Top = 1, @Failed = 1
```

Back in Chapter 4, we looked at the many reports in Grid View you could see the plan_ids and query_ids. If you are looking to see the sp_BlitzQueryStore data for a query you have identified from those reports, then you can use the code from Listings 10-15 and 10-16 to pull the data out of Query Store.

Listing 10-15. Return data by plan_id

```
EXEC sp_BlitzQueryStore @DatabaseName = 'AdventureWorks',
    @PlanIdFilter = 3356
```

Listing 10-16. Return data by query_id

```
EXEC sp_BlitzQueryStore @DatabaseName = 'AdventureWorks',
    @QueryIdFilter = 2958
```

Other parameters you can specify include the following in Table 10-1.

Table 10-1. *sp_BlitzQueryStore parameters*

Parameter name	Data type	Default
@Help	bit	0
@MinimumExecutionCount	int	NULL
@DurationFilter	decimal(38, 4)	NULL
@ExportToExcel	bit	0
@HideSummary	bit	0
@SkipXML	bit	0
@Debug	bit	0
@ExpertMode	bit	0
@Version	varchar(30)	NULL
@VersionDate	datetime	NULL
@VersionCheckMode	bit	0

Conclusion

Community tools prove to enhance our ability to use Query Store. dbatools lets us configure and check the settings of Query Store across multiple databases and servers with ease. sp_BlitzQueryStore lets you harvest the data in Query Store in a different format than the reports shown in Chapter 4 and can be useful for finding out what your top queries are for each metric quickly and what your busiest periods of times are for each metric. Finally, it allows you to track data for a stored procedure, query_id, or plan_id that you have identified you want to investigate further.

Index

A

ad-hoc queries, 57, 58, 69, 74, 144, 145
AdventureWorks database, 151, 170, 203, 206
Automatic plan correction
    automatic tuning (*see* Automatic tuning)
    behavior, 170
    capabilities, 169
    concepts, 169
    regression (*see* Regression)
Automatic plan regression correction
        (APRC), 47, 61, 62
    disable T-SQL, 62
    enable T-SQL, 61
Automatic tuning, 177–178, 181
    Azure portal, 178–180
    CurrentState value, 182
    performance, 182
    regression, 182
    T-SQL command, 180

B

Baseline, 2
    catalog views, 3
    compare workload back, 138
    create, 136
    definition, 136
    establish, 135
    overall resource consumption, 2, 3
    performance, 4

C

Catalog view, Query store, 56
Compiled stored procedures, 47, 60, 70
Configuration options
    cache per query, 54
    capture queries, 53
    changing, GUI, 55, 56
    CUSTOM mode, 53
    database renaming, 59
    data clean up, 52
    data flush interval, 51
    drop /create, 58
    interval data, 52
    maximum storage size, 51
    operational mode, 50
    parameterization, 57, 58
    STALE_QUERY_THRESHOLD_DAYS, 50
    trace flag, 59
    wait statistics, 54
Copy-DbaQueryStoreConfig, 206
    database, 206
CPU, queries, 124

D

Database Platform as a Service
        (PaaS), 47, 48
Database properties, 137
Data Definition Language (DDL), 34
Data flush interval, 51, 59

215

E

F

G, H

I, J, K, L

M

U, V

W, X, Y, Z